The Terre Haute
YWCA Story
As Reported in the Newspapers

Pat and Dale Bringman

Pat and Dale Bringman
The Terre Haute YWCA Story
As Reported in the Newspapers

ISBN: 978-1-955154-27-7

Published by Valley Publishing Co.,
a division of MAYS Multimedia

VALLEY
PUBLISHING
COMPANY

www.vpcbooks.com

Detroit, Michigan, USA Printed in the
United States of America

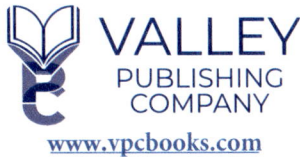

Terre Haute YWCA through the Years

Introduction
The Terre Haute
YWCA Story
As Reported in the Newspapers

The Terre Haute YWCA (Young Women's Christian Association) proudly served the Terre Haute, Indiana community for over 100 years. The "Y," as it was often called, offered a broad spectrum of services and programs created to enrich the lives of individuals of all age groups and socio-economic backgrounds.

Since its inception in 1902, the Terre Haute YWCA, a non-profit entity, served a dual role: providing multiple benefits for its members and sponsoring wide-ranging programs for the general community. While various sources were consulted to describe these roles, most of the information was found in Terre Haute newspapers. This book represents a brief history and review of the Association, the names and key roles that many people played in the organization's development and operation, and the array of services the YWCA provided to the community for more than a century.

The number of people directly connected to the origin and evolution of the Terre Haute YWCA is far too many to count. After all, there were administrators, directors, instructors, and uncountable volunteers who contributed to the overall achievements of the YWCA, all of whom deserve credit or a mention for their respective contributions. For all who were not included, we apologize. The omission was not intentional.

Acknowledgments

This project began with a request from Cindi Monds, executive director of the Vigo County YWCA in Terre Haute, asking for a historical timeline to be displayed on an empty wall at the YMCA. The research conducted for that timeline led directly to this book.

As with any project such as this, the number of contributors is quite large; however, the following individuals deserve special recognition.

To Suzy Quick and Mary Add Baker of the Vigo County Historical Museum; for their valuable help in locating historical documents chronicling the early years of the YWCA.

To the staff of the Special Collections of the Vigo County Library; a special thanks to Sean Eislie, Janet Thatcher, Logan Knight, and Sloane Engle for their assistance and endless patience.

To the numerous individuals with past and current connections to the YWCA and later, the YMCA, who have provided critical insights into the operation of a valuable community asset. Linda Hoolehan, Martha Crossen, and Becky Buse were particularly helpful in providing materials from their personal collections. We thank them all.

To Mark Bennett: Thanks, from the community, for his continued efforts in keeping the news of the Ys publicized and for his encouragement for this project.

To John Becker: Thanks for his assistance and sharing his extensive library of Terre Haute history.

To Tim Crumrin, local historian and author, for his guidance in directing this project through the hurdles of publishing.

To Dorothy Jerse: We are especially grateful for her friendship and support. We were fortunate to have the guidance of someone with extensive first-hand experience with the YWCA. Her fondness for the Terre Haute YWCA and its role in the community is unmatched.

Table of Contents

Chapter 1 Meeting a Growing Need: The Founding
The First YWCAs

For the average person living in the United States or Europe during the mid-nineteenth century, surviving was a continuing struggle. For men, whether working in agriculture or in one of the many industries that arose with the growth of the industrial revolution, securing food and shelter left little time for other pursuits. For women, the struggles of maintaining the house while dealing with large families simply were physically and mentally draining. Self-improvement and quality-of-life goals were usually out of reach for all but the wealthy.

Several reform movements arose in the early 1800s to address existing social ills. Abolition of slavery, temperance, women's rights, prison reform, and child labor reform were common targets of various organized groups. Reform groups were usually evangelical protestants who continued to work toward improving living conditions well into the early 1900s. Among these reform groups were organized chapters of the Young Men's Christian Association (YMCA) and the Young Women's Christian Association (YWCA) organized to empower lives across a broad cross-section of society.

A young women's association was organized in London to find housing for nurses returning from the Crimean War. Around the same time, another group organized Bible study and prayer circles. The two groups merged in 1877 and became the Young Women's Christian Association (YWCA).

The first YWCA in the United States was founded in Boston in 1866. The movement continued to grow in industrial cities and on college and university campuses throughout the United States.

The turn of the century found Terre Haute, Indiana, a prosperous city with many industries. The rural population was migrating to industrial centers like Terre Haute, and the YWCA movement was especially concerned about the overall welfare of women from rural areas. Efforts toward providing safe and affordable room and board, along with opportunities for self-improvement, followed.

Terre Haute YWCAs

The first record of the YWCA in Terre Haute, as published in the *Normal Advance*, Indiana State Normal School's yearbook, indicated that a student association of the YWCA "received a certificate as a charter member of the new national organization under the National Board" in 1885. Coincidently, a chapter of the YMCA was organized in Terre Haute simultaneously. In addition to the YWCA's usual support for improving the conditions of young women, the upstart student association concentrated on a mechanism to offer appropriate housing for Indiana State Normal School women.

Indiana State Normal YWCA
414 North Sixth Street

The 1902-1903 *Indiana State Normal School Catalogue* announced that the student YWCA had rented a large house at 414 North 6th Street (the present location of the Hulman Memorial Student Union) to provide headquarters for the organization, along with room and board accommodations for twenty-seven young women. The rooms were rented at five dollars per month, and "table board" (meals) was provided at the regular price of club board in Terre Haute – two dollars per week. With cooperation from the Indiana State Normal School, faculty member Mary J. Anderson provided supervision. Around 1910, a general secretary was hired to supervise the houses. The young women leased other locations. A 1912 Terre Haute city directory indicates that a location at 520 North Center Street served as the student YWCA; the 1912 issue of the *Normal Advance* refers to the YW Association House at 428 North Center Street. Housing of this type, called "boarding clubs," served women of Indiana State Normal School until Reeve Hall opened on campus in 1925.

As early as 1893, Indiana State Normal School's support of the student YWCA was evidenced by the planning for an academic building on the Normal School's campus. The assignment of internal spaces listed the third floor as the location for the student YWCA and YMCA. This support continued when on April 26, 1918, Indiana State Normal School purchased property and opened a Student Building at 671 Eagle Street. This purchase was a short-term alternative to a planned new Student Building (Student Union). Still, due to economic hard times and sacrifice for the war effort, the new building was delayed until the late thirties. Among the house's features were four large upstairs rooms for committee meetings, YMCA and YWCA meeting rooms, and a library room. Years later, with on-campus housing offered by Indiana State Normal, the student YWCA disbanded around 1933.

**Indiana State Normal School
North Hall**

**Indiana State Normal School
Student Building**

Shortly after the turn of the 20th Century, several women convening at the home of Mrs. Virginia Mack on North 8th Street organized the Terre Haute YWCA, the third location in Indiana. Mrs. Joseph (Mary I.) Jenckes served as the first Terre Haute YWCA president from 1902 until 1904. After moving to Indianapolis, Jenckes remained active in social organizations, served as a board member of the YWCA for several years, and was the state chairman of the YWCA in 1909. Jenckes died in November 1933 at the age of eighty-four. Her sister-in-law, Virginia Jenckes, was also a pioneer of women's rights and served as Indiana's first woman United States Representative for three terms on Capitol Hill from March 1933 until January 1939. The Jenckes family originally owned the land now occupied by Highland Lawn Cemetery. Mary Jenckes is buried near the family marker on the site of the family's first home, built in 1820.

Jenckes Memorial – Highland Lawn Cemetery
Terre Haute, Indiana

In the fall of 1902, the YWCA leased a house from Mrs. A. Louisa Early at 664 Ohio Street (later the Ohio Building) to provide meals and limited housing. (The same year, the YMCA occupied a house a few doors away at 644 Ohio). The house was a beginning, although a serious limitation was its inadequate space for residents or visitors; it was limited to just five women.

On May 30, 1904, the Terre Haute YWCA was formally incorporated. It was the third city YWCA incorporated in Indiana. Sixty-six members of the board of directors signed the incorporation papers. Their purpose read,

"The improvement of the physical, social, intellectual, and spiritual condition of young women."

Mrs. I.H.C. Royse was one of the charter members and served as president from 1904 through 1921.

Mrs. I.H.C. Royse
2nd President YWCA

On February 13, 1907, the general assembly of the State of Indiana reacted to an emergency regarding the State's YWCAs and YMCAs. It was unclear whether the incorporation of the Associations and their right to hold real estate was legal. A remedy was enacted that detailed rules governing the incorporation of both the YMCAs and the YWCAs. (See Appendix A for the complete act.)

For the first several years after incorporation, the Terre Haute YWCA's efforts were concentrated on employed women and those women attending school away from home. Until Reeve Hall, a residence hall at Indiana State Normal School was built in 1925, the YWCA worked to solve housing problems for hundreds of female students. In 1902, lodging was provided 209 times for women from out of town. In addition, 29,989 meals were served to people at an average cost of fourteen cents. The total attendance at vesper services was 1,975; at physical culture classes, 1,476. Other classes included China painting, embroidery, literature, grammar, history, and wood carving.

Costs from 1904 were reported as follows: membership was one dollar per year for regular members and five dollars per year for maintaining members. An example of dining room prices from the 1904 menu includes chicken pie for five cents, mashed potatoes for three cents, and tea, coffee, cocoa, or milk for three cents.

The YWCA instituted an early outreach program with Emma Moore, the organization's general secretary, who spent many noon hours at local factories in study groups with female employees. The *Spectator's* October 8, 1905 issue noted, "The YWCA has filled such an important niche in the circle of institutions, having for their several objectives the betterment of the community in general, that few can understand why we were so long without it." The efforts of the YWCA were expanding rapidly, causing women to look for larger and better facilities. Housing needs were especially critical because the present facility could accommodate only five women overnight.

Another announcement in 1905 advertised an employment bureau had been added with Mrs. William Mack serving as chair. Women searching for work were to "send requests with recommendations to the Association, 664 Ohio Street."

The *Ten-Year Report* of the Terre Haute YWCA (1912) summarized the varied activities and locations during the early years.

> "There were the following departments: The religious side of the Association has been prominent. A vesper service is held every Sunday at 4:00 p.m., and a number of Bible Classes are held each year. Noon meetings have been conducted in five factories. Some educational work has been done, and much has been made of the social work. The physical work was carried on for a year in one of the living rooms of the building with one piece of apparatus – a jumping standard. The second and third years, the Wiley High School kindly tendered the use of their gymnasium and apparatus. The fourth year the basement of the First M.E. Church was leased, the fifth year, the basement of Centenary Church was leased, and the sixth year's work was done in the home of the YWCA, the old library building. The present director is Miss Edna Price Brown, a graduate of the New Haven Normal School of Gymnastics who is beginning her third year.
>
> There were four instructors during the first two years and two during the last four years.
>
> The Lunch Department has been an important feature where business girls could buy a palatable meal at moderate cost. One meal a day was served the first year, and then to accommodate business girls who were in evening classes, suppers were served.
>
> The lunch began with an attendance of about forty a day and has steadily increased until at present about one hundred and fifty persons are served each day. A large number of students have waited tables for their board, and in this way helped themselves through school."

Obtaining an Appropriate Facility

Before a permanent location could be obtained for the Terre Haute YWCA, the leased Ohio Street location was sold to the Spang Reality company, forcing the Association to find new quarters. A temporary location was found in a structure originally built as the Universalist Church, located at 119 North 8th Street (across from the current Indiana State University parking garage). Vacated by the city library, occupying it as a temporary solution to space needs, this building served as the YWCA's headquarters and location for programs. In addition, from April 1907 until the opening of permanent facilities in September 1908, a house at 202 South 8th Street was obtained for a women's residence. This rooming house accommodated a maximum of nineteen women.

Universalist Church

As the board considered a permanent facility, it was apparent that serious fundraising would be required. One of the first efforts was by the business girls themselves, canvassing self-supporting women. Their efforts raised $750.00. Another of the finance committee's projects to build the reserve fund was the publication and sale of the *Up-To-Date Cookbook*. An entry from the *Spectator* stated, "The YWCA cookbook is still on sale and will be until every housekeeper, present and prospective, is supplied with a copy. It is a two-dollar book for one dollar. It is a complete and valuable work. These books can be secured at the Association house or most of the leading stores." The recipes were contributed by prominent residents of Terre Haute and covered a wide- range of dishes from "soup to nuts." (The recipe for turtle soup even included instructions on preparing the turtle.)

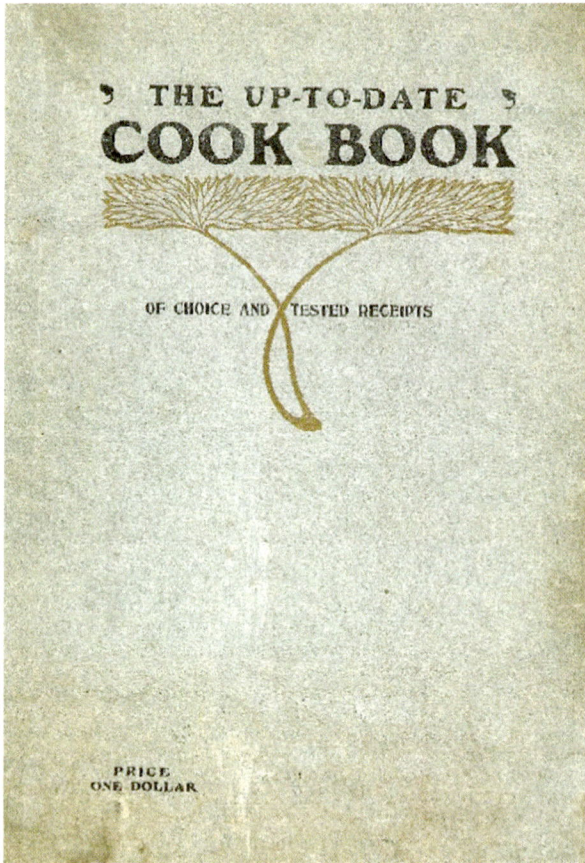

Cookbook Cover

On January 3, 1907, the board of directors agreed to purchase the property at 121 North 7th Street from Mrs. Nancy M. Westfall as a site for a proposed new building. Indianapolis architects Foltz and Parker drew up plans for a three-story building. From a collection of unidentified newspaper clippings, Mr. I.H.C. Royse, husband of the YWCA president and chair of the Building Fund Committee, reported that the young women had raised $11,000 to build a good home for the Association. However, $50,000 more would be necessary. (Mr. Royse also served as president of the Terre Haute YMCA beginning in 1875).

It was further reported that ten committees would be formed, each consisting of ten to twelve influential members of the community. It should be noted the committee rosters read like a Who's Who of Terre Haute society. For one week, the committees met at a noon luncheon to organize the whirlwind effort to solicit support from the Terre Haute business community. The campaign raised $44,000, and a $30,000 mortgage was taken out to cover anticipated costs to finish the building.

Campaign Committee Leaders

The *Terre Haute Tribune* reported on Sunday, April 11, 1948, in a column titled "Terre Haute Forty Years Ago Today"

> **"that the building committee of the Young Women's Christian Association Tuesday morning let the contract for the Association's new home to H. G. Stillwell of Lafayette on his bid of $42,000. That total was exclusive of lighting, heating, plumbing, and electrical work. The building will be made of colonial brick with trimmings of the lighter shade of gray terra cotta. The foundation will be of green river stone."**

The plans for the interior consisted of offices, reception parlors, dining rooms, and a kitchen on the first floor. The second floor featured conference rooms and a large assembly hall with a stage. The third floor was a young women's dormitory accommodating forty to sixty residents. The basement was to house the swimming pool, showers, and gymnasium. Work was to begin at once and to be completed by October 1.

121 North Seventh Street

On June 4, 1908, the cornerstone was laid with "imposing ceremonies." Mrs. Lilly M Strong, the state YWCA secretary who had helped start the movement in Terre Haute, was the speaker. She said," Strangers should be able to feel they are as welcome at this YWCA home as they are at their own firesides, and that it should be a social and spiritual sanctuary." The day-to-day supervision of the facility was assigned to Emma B. Moore as the "general secretary," a title used before "executive director" came into use.

The third-floor rooms were soon occupied by young women, many students attending Indiana State Normal. Rent for a furnished room was $3.00 per week and was to be shared with two or sometimes three residents.

Fundraising continued. A. J. Steen, a local businessman and real estate developer turned over seventy-eight lots at 13th and College Streets, a development called Victorine Park near Montrose Church and Montrose School, to be sold to benefit the building fund. Prospective buyers were there at dawn, and the choice lots had been sold by noon. Men volunteered as salesmen. About $10,000 more was raised.

YWCA Building
121 North 7th Street

The swimming pool in the basement was a particularly important addition to the programs of the Association. These women were ahead of their time. They built the only indoor pool in Terre Haute at the time; for many years, it was the only indoor swimming pool regularly inspected for safety by the Terre Haute Water Works Company. In addition to its use by YWCA members, Indiana State Normal School classes utilized the pool and gymnasium for both men's and women's activities for several years.

Gymnasium

Reflections from Ann Prox, a long-time member and patron:

"I started my swimming career learning to swim at the YWCA on North 7th Street in the fall of 1955. My memory of the pool is it was like a cave. The sides of the pool were high, and you could only get out on the ladder. In 1984, I started "stretch and tone" at the current Y building. In the fall of 1989, I started swimming in the new pool!"

Swim Lesson for Young Girls

More Young Swimmers

Later the YWCA expanded its programs to include the city's first local typing and domestic science classes. It is noted that Mrs. Boyd Miller, a member of the national board, mentioned in a 1949 speech that "the early typing classes offered by the country's YWCAs were the occasion of newspaper editorials which expressed a fear that the strain of operating such a heavy machine would be detrimental to the young ladies."

Dorm Rooms for Residents

Dorm Rooms for Residents

Related Materials

BOARD OF DIRECTORS

OF THE

Young Women's Christian Association

Mrs. I. H. C. Royse, President.
Mrs. Dan N. Davis, 1st Vice-President.
Mrs. Frank McKeen, 2nd Vice-President.
Mrs. H. P. Townley, 3rd Vice-President.
Mrs. J. H. Keyes, 4th Vice-President.
Mrs. G. A. Conzman, Treasurer.
Mrs. Walter C. Clark, Recording Secretary.
Mrs. R. S. Tennant, Corresponding Secretary.

Mrs. Allyn G. Adams.	Mrs. M. H. Waters.
Mrs. J. M. Rogers.	Mrs. Emil Froeb.
Mrs. A. H. Donham.	Mrs. Eva Hollinger.
Mrs. J. M. Hedges.	Mrs. E. W. Kemp.
Mrs. W. O. Jenkins.	Mrs. W. R. Mail.
Mrs. Amanda Mack.	Mrs. B. V. Marshall.
Mrs. W. A. McBeth.	Miss Helen Minshall.
Mrs. C. F. Miller.	Mrs. Fred Smith.
Mrs. Walker Schell.	Mrs. J. A. Wickersham.
Mrs. John Warren.	Mrs. E. F. Rodenbeck.
Mrs. W. H. Wiley.	Mrs. A. J. Crawford.
Mrs. E. B. McAllister.	Mrs. B. G. Hudnut.
Mrs. Wilbur Topping.	Mrs. Charles Minshall.
Mrs. W. C. Isbell.	

Miss Emma B. Moore, General Secretary.
Miss Carrie A. Smith, House Secretary.
Miss Jeannie A. Randolph, Extension Secretary and Physical
    Director.

**1904 Board of Directors
and Officers of YWCA**

Y. W. C. A. Work for 1904

MEMBERSHIP

QUALIFICATIONS: GOOD MORAL CHARACTER

FEES:

Regular Members.......... $1.00 per year
Sustaining Members........ $5.00 per year
Life Members.............. $100.00

WORK THAT HAS BEEN DONE

Meals served to 29,989 people at an average cost of 14 cents.

Provided lodging 209 times for women and girls from out of town.

Vesper services:

Average attendance.......... 49
Total attendance........... 1975
Classes in Physical Culture... 184
Attendance.................. 1476

WORK DONE BY GENERAL SECRETARY

Number of Bible Class Sessions 129
Attendance at Bible Class Sessions 1308
Meetings at Factories 115
Number of Socials.......... 17
Attendance at Socials 545
Calls made by Secretaries.... 72
Letters and Postals written.. 824
Announcements distributed... 3838

PRIVILEGES

Eligibility to Classes.

Circulating Library and Reading Room with daily papers and all leading magazines.

Rest Room with couches and easy chairs.

Large Parlor with piano and music box.

Classes in Literature, Grammar, History, Embroidery, China Painting, Physical Culture and Wood Carving.

Guest Room with two beds.

———

Frequently young women travelling alone or strangers are welcomed to the Home at any hour, where they may remain over night for a nominal sum.

**Review of accomplishments
from Cookbook**

Cookbook Liner Page 1905

Advertisements from Cookbook

IDEAS PICKED UP

"A pint is a pound the world around."

* * *

Kerosene poured down waste pipes is a thorough purifier, and lessens one's plumber bill.

* * *

To prevent the dough from adhering to the spoon in making drop cakes, place the spoon after each cake in a cup of cold water.
—*Mrs. John C. Warren.*

* * *

A small butter plate, put in the bottom of a kettle of jam when cooking will prevent the fruit from sticking to the bottom of the kettle.

* * *

Good meat should present a marble appearance, from an inter-mixture of fat and muscle. This shows that the animal has been well fed.

* * *

In boiling water for drinking, just allow the water to come to the boiling point. Boiling a long time makes the water flat and tasteless.

* * *

Hot water containing a little chloride of lime poured down the waste pipes every few days during the hot season will prevent bad odors; the cause of such odors often produces typhoid fever.

* * *

In the early summer when apples first appear in the markets, they are small and not well formed. In peeling them and remov-ing seeds but little is left. Wash carefully and cut in two the apples, and put them on to cook with hot water. As soon as the apples are soft, but not mushy, put them through a colander tak-ing out all seeds and skins; then put them back on the stove again, add sugar, and cook not more than fifteen minutes. This saves the apple.

Helpful Hints included in the
Cookbook

**Indiana State Normal School YWCA
cabinet – from 1908 *Normal Advance***

Mrs. Joseph S. Jenckes of Indianapolis has sent the
Y.W.C.A. an excellent framed picture of herself. It
hangs in the reading room, representing the first
president of the association. Mrs. Jenckes' work will
go down in the history of the organization. She is a
magnetic woman of fine address and much
enthusiasm.

Saturday Spectator – 7-14-1906

Chapter 2 Serving Communities Near and Far
1910s through the 1940s

The initial need that drove the formation of the Terre Haute YWCA was to have safe housing for young women joining the nation's workforce. However, that role soon expanded beyond a single issue. In 1902, the YWCA's stated purpose indicated a broad offering of valuable services. The Association recognized these services during the planning for the new building, which included more than housing. This vision was proven by the varied amenities of the YWCA during the early to mid-1910s, as indicated by the following brief samples from newspapers, including The *Saturday Spectator* and *Terre Haute Star*.

1913

- Mrs. J.C. Warren and Mrs. H.J. Wanner will represent the Terre Haute YWCA at the annual convention in Chicago, October 17 to 19.

- The YWCA campaign to raise $25,000 got off to a fine start Saturday with over $6,000 subscribed and several other large pledges made. The total later reported to be short, only reaching $5,656.35.

1914

- Mrs. John B. Wisely will conduct the YWCA vesper services Sunday afternoon with Gertrude Haupt to play a violin solo.

- The YWCA building is being redecorated and no meals will be served there until next Monday noon.

1915

- About 150 girls attended the meeting of the Business Girl's Bible League at the YWCA this past week.

- A turkey supper was given Tuesday from 5 to 7 at the YWCA with the industrial classes also meeting.

1917

- YWCA girls have turned to camp life to escape the city's hot breath on summer nights with the camp located west of Terre Haute.

- The local council of Women's Clubs met Wednesday at the YWCA with good attendance reported.

- The monthly meeting of the Women's Christian Temperance Union will be held Sunday at 3:00 at the YWCA.

The meeting rooms of the YWCA provided a welcoming environment for a wide variety of women's organizations. Dozens of groups met regularly there for decades. The extent of the building's use was described in a Saturday Spectator article on April 3, 1920 "As a gathering place and headquarters for committee meetings, the YWCA is becoming more and more popular. One day this week, during the space of one short hour, there were nine different committee meetings in session with more than a hundred persons in attendance and every available spot on the lower floors taken."

One of the characteristics of city life in Terre Haute during the 1910s was described in a *Saturday Spectator* article published October 18, 1913. "The YWCA building is only five years old, but is located in the worst soft coal zone of the city. Naturally, the walls are black. A pressing need is to have the walls painted, but the board of managers is held on a leash by the interest on the building debt of $20,000 and have no funds for this necessary work." The article continued by suggesting that individual volunteers might assist.

Teenage Girls

An early concern of the YWCA was the quality of life of young girls from diverse environments and cultures. This often limiting background was worsened by the effects of World War I. Inflation caused by expanded government expenditures caused layoffs, and the increase in unemployment was worsened by the simultaneous northern migration of poor southerners. The influx of people to the already crowded cities often led to squalid conditions. One result of those conditions was the YWCA's formation of the Girl Reserve Movement to serve young girls between the ages of twelve and eighteen with the following stated purpose:

> **"The object of the Girl Reserve Movement, in direct accordance with the purpose of the YWCA, is to make a contribution to those elements in the life of a girl which set free the ideals and convictions that help a girl to live as a Christian of her age should live, and aid her to put into practice in her community her standards of Christian living. It endeavors to help a girl grow through normal, natural activities into those habits, insights, and ideals which will make her a responsible, eager woman, capable and ready to develop and share group expressions which are making defective the purpose of God in the world."**

In 1916, the Terre Haute YWCA Girl Reserve Clubs for teenage girls were formed in the city high schools. Terre Haute claimed 623 members in Garfield, Gerstmeyer, Classical, State, Wiley, McLean, Wilson, Deming, and Hook schools.

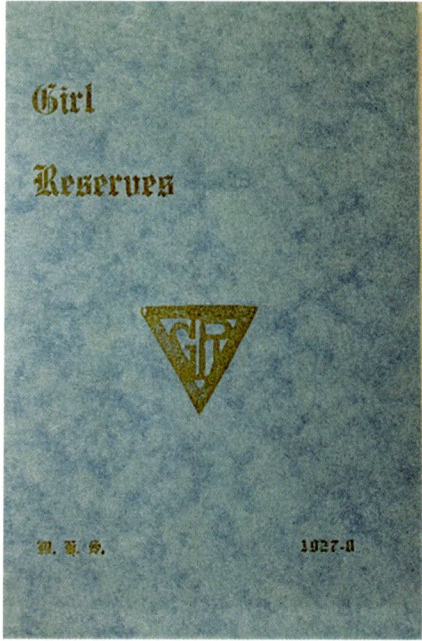

Girl Reserve Poster

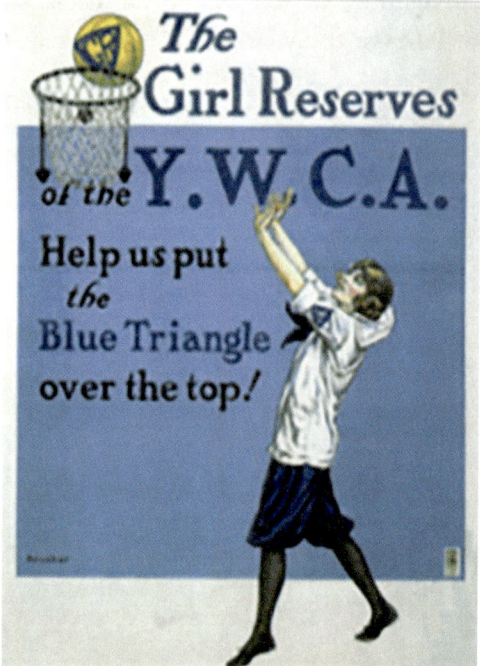

Girl Reserve Poster

The first Girl Scout troop in Terre Haute was also organized by the YWCA in the 1910s, specifically by Ida Probst. The *Saturday Spectator* described early scouting activities. On August 2, 1917, it reported, "Girl Scout Day Camps are being held this week and next at Deming Park. Mrs. Pat Bailey, the director, reports that ninety girls are attending daily." A few years later, on July 3, 1920, they shared, "Girl scouts have been holding forth at the YWCA camp this week with Miss Mildred Kelly, with some of the girls' mothers and Miss Margaret Markle chaperoning at various times. Next week the Aokaya Campfire Girls, who have as their guardian, Miss Mary Amour, will enjoy an outing at camp. Dewey Lake delegates, federation officers, and club presidents will spend the weekend at Camp Lafalot."

The first Blue Triangle Clubs for girls in Terre Haute were formed at Wiley and Garfield Schools in 1919. As reported in the *Saturday Spectator* on November 27, 1920, these clubs were under the direction of Miss Margaret Gardner, who wasn't more than 19 years old. At the time of this report, Wiley had 117 members from the school, Garfield had nearly 100, and a group from State Normal High School was completing the application to become members. In addition, a group from the Girls Vocational School and two groups of Girl Scouts were pursuing membership. At the time of the *Saturday Spectator* article, approximately 500 girls were organized into these clubs.

Blue Triangle Cover

There was general enthusiasm for the Blue Triangle program noted by Mrs. John Warren, the YWCA chairman of the girls' work department. In particular, she said, "The best part of it, however, has to do with the training received by the individual members. It is a revelation to look in on one of the business meetings in progress. In fact, it might be a revelation to men who are in the business of holding business meetings. Strict parliamentary procedure is observed in the routine work. Girls have previously had little training on how a meeting should be conducted. Then too, the round table discussions which follow are lively and intelligent affairs." Teachers in the participating schools acted as advisees to the popular clubs. They were expecting enrollments to double to nearly 1,000 members quickly.

Adult Clubs

The Terre Haute Business and Professional Women's Club was organized in 1917 at the YWCA, two years before the formation of the National Federation of Business and Professional Women's Clubs, with which it was later affiliated. Within a few years, the Terre Haute Club helped organize a second similar organization: The Vigo County Business and Professional Women's Club.

World War I

During World War I (WWI), the YWCA took pride in being the only women's organization officially affiliated with the Commission on Training Camp Activities (CTCA) and the United War Work Campaign (UWWC). This affiliation caused friction among women's religious groups from the Knights of Columbus, the Jewish Welfare Board, and the Salvation Army when the CTCA refused to fund them. It was felt the leaders of the UWWC glossed over the concern of the women in religious minorities, describing the distinctly Protestant organization as the representative of all American women.

In addition to a wide variety of domestic activities to assist the war effort, the YWCA offered assistance to American women serving overseas as nurses, stenographers, telephone operators, and relief workers.

WWI Poster

One of the YWCA's contributions during WWI included the operation of "Hostess Houses" located near army training bases. The houses were established to provide a home away from home for family members visiting trainees. An influenza pandemic was raging at the time, which added stress to those working at the camps. The following account was reported by Miss Margaret Langford of Terre Haute, who served at a Hostess House near Camp Riley in Louisville, Kentucky. She described the conditions at the camp of 10,000 soldiers in November 1918 as visitors arrived to see their sick friends and relatives.

"The six women in the Hostess House started out to take care of the crowds by themselves, but the task was impossible. Two hundred persons were accommodated overnight in the small building by placing cots in every available corner. Tents were put up in the yard, soldiers were sent from the camp to help with the cleaning and cooking, and distance messages, and the Western Union sent a special operator to the house to take charge of wires." Miss Langford added, "everyone wears a mask and we are a funny looking sight. Things both pathetic and amusing are happening all the time. Don't know what we would have done if we could not have seen the comical side of many of the incidents."

(It's difficult not to see the connections across the decades, as a similar health crisis has impacted the United States and the world at the time of this writing, Fall 2020).

Hostess House Cartoon

Hostess Houses continued to be active, extending their contributions through WWII. In May 1945, Miss Letha Coakley served as a Hostess House librarian at the Wakeman General Hospital at Camp Atterbury (near Columbus, Indiana). The previous years, she had been a school librarian in Sullivan, Indiana.

Organizations that began within the YWCA

A number of activities and services, which began in the YWCA to meet a specific need, developed into separate and strong organizations. The National Association of Travelers Aid Societies, the National Federation of Business and Professional Women's Clubs, the International Migration Service, and the National Institute of Immigrant Welfare all originated within the YWCA and became independent movements with no organic connection with the Association.

Mortgage is Burned

As the decade of the 1910s ended, the mortgage on the YWCA building at 121 North 7th Street was burned in the front parlor fireplace, as part of an impressive ceremony on October 14, 1919. As Mrs. I.H.C. Royse lit the legal papers, all present burst into singing "Praise God from Whom All Blessings Flow." The $30,000 mortgage had been paid off bit by bit during the ten years following the building's construction. The date also marked the seventy-seventh birthday of Mrs. Amanda Mack, at whose home the organization had begun.

Traveler Assistance

A *Terre Haute Tribune* article from February 1924, emphasized the concern of the YWCA for travelers, especially young women who were arriving in Terre Haute in increasing numbers. The article noted,

> **"The need for a traveler's aid bureau in Terre Haute, as a part of the YWCA, was discussed at a luncheon given Tuesday by Mrs. W. G. Clark and Mrs. Harry Zimmerman**

for the publicity committee of the organization. Instances are told of the number of young women who are coming into Terre Haute from surrounding towns and foreign countries, and the danger that they meet in having no one to meet them or see that they are established. One story told of two young girls who had come here searching for work. When they arrived, they asked the way to the YWCA and followed the directions to 7th and Wabash. There they asked directions from a policeman, who informed them he had never heard of the YWCA. Finally, they located the building and were taken care of. The secretary helped them find employment and saw that they were cared for until they became acquainted and able to care for themselves."

Miss Julia Van Arsdale, general secretary, continued and told of the large number of calls the YW has to meet trains, especially the one which arrives shortly after midnight. She expressed the feeling, "that because there was no official at the station, no estimate could be made of the number who comes into Terre Haute without friends. The Travelers' Aid not only is for young girls, but for all travelers, as it furnishes a reliable source of information and general helpfulness. What is desired is an increase in the budget of the organization, which will help pay the salary of a motherly person who will spend her time at the station and then do follow-up work in the cases of strange girls coming into Terre Haute."

Another example described the work of the secretary of the YWCA meeting trains with identification sent to her regarding foreign-born girls and women who are either changing trains here or coming into the city to marry or become domestics. At the luncheon, it was reported that a Mrs. Hutton had met five girls from Germany, arriving in Terre Haute to work for Mr. and Mrs. Schwerdt as either domestics or work in their bakery. To meet the continuing need, a Traveler's Aid Association was established in the YWCA and operated several years there until moving to a home of its own.

Services in the Building

For the entire history of the YWCA, maintaining health and fitness was a core objective. In addition to continued efforts to improve various sectors of community life, the need for individual health was continually supported by access to the facility and the personnel. The cartoon below is a sample of that promotion.

Fitness Cartoon

One of the most popular features of the Terre Haute YWCA building and a major source of revenue was the cafeteria. At one time, both men and women stood in long lines stretching down 7th Street at the noon hour, with waiting times reported as often as long as twenty minutes or more. However, the cafeteria's popularity raised concern among some YWCA members. Their concern was that business men who could afford to eat elsewhere were taking the dining spots of working women, the population the YWCA's cafeteria was meant to serve. Mrs. Taylor, the general secretary, responded that the men ate more but paid more; therefore, they subsidized meals for young women.

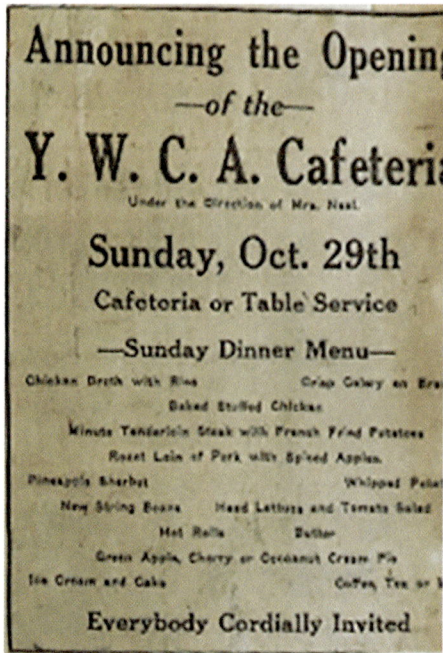

Announcing the Opening

—of the—

Y. W. C. A. Cafeteria

Under the direction of Mrs. Neal

Sunday, Oct. 29th

Cafeteria or Table Service

—Sunday Dinner Menu—

Chicken Broth with Rice · · · · · · Crisp Celery on Bread
Baked Stuffed Chicken
Minute Tenderloin Steak with French Fried Potatoes
Roast Loin of Pork with Spiced Apples
Pineapple Sherbet · · · · · · Whipped Potatoes
New String Beans · · · Head Lettuce and Tomato Salad
Hot Rolls · · · · · · Butter
Green Apple, Cherry or Cocoanut Cream Pie
Ice Cream and Cake · · · · · · Coffee, Tea or Milk

Everybody Cordially Invited

Cafeteria Opening

Budgets in the 1930s

For several years in the late 1920s and early '30s, the annual budgets were approximately $45,000. Income for each year varied based on the economy, but usually left between $5,000 -- $10,000 to be raised by special campaigns. Limitations on income were especially severe during the depression years. In March of 1937, civic leaders of Terre Haute noted that the budget had been restricted to the bare necessities and was inadequate to meet critical needs. The 1937 campaign to raise $112,000 for the YWCA was the first to be conducted by the men of Terre Haute.

World War II

Just before the onset of America's involvement in World War II, President Franklin D. Roosevelt sought to unite several associations to lift the morale of our military and encourage support on the home front. Those entities – the Salvation Army, Young Men's Christian Association,

Young Women's Christian Association, National Catholic Community Services, National Travelers Aid Association, and the National Jewish Welfare Board – became the United Services Organizations, or USO, on February 4, 1941. Terre Haute headquarters was located at 674 Wabash Avenue with four USO centers in the city, with one at the YWCA. The Association created a lounge on the second floor for the young women in the residence, and the first floor was given to the USO Service Club. The gymnasium was used for USO dances. Special events were held in larger auditoriums in town.

USO Group -- 1943

USO Dance – 1943

The YWCA was involved in a wide variety of services and programs during WWII to support those serving overseas and those helping at home. As might be expected, cooperation and resource-sharing among service agencies were common at this time. A prime example was the cooperation between the Red Cross and its activities, often hosted by the YWCA.

On March 6, 1943, the National Panhellenic Conference announced that a class of women "had enrolled for the Red Cross First Aid classes to be held every Tuesday evening at the YWCA from 7:30 p.m. until 9:30 p.m.." Similar announcements were made at the time for "two new classes in Red Cross home nursing to be held at the YWCA."

Knitting Group at YWCA - 1943

Sewing Group at YWCA - 1943

Still another contribution to the war effort was described in the *Saturday Spectator* in October 1942: "The local Red Cross is announcing that they are now well supplied with yarn for knitting, and it can be obtained at the YWCA. An urgent plea is made that knitting begins at once, in order that warm garments be completed and ready for shipment before the coming winter months. The Red Cross knitting groups meet on Wednesday and Friday, and many more knitters are needed, if our boys are to be supplied with sufficient warm clothing during the next year."

The Women's Army Auxiliary Corps (WAAC) was formed on May 15, 1942, and renamed the Women's Army Corps on July 1, 1943. The Terre Haute girls and women contributed from the beginning. Only a month after formation, a June 1942 article in the *Spectator* stated, "An announcement was made Thursday by Lieut. Olive Moeckel of a forthcoming meeting of girls in the WAAC. The meeting will be held on Tuesday evening, June 2 at 8:00, and guardians are cordially invited to attend."

WAC Sendoff Party

Overseas Wives Club

After the war, an Overseas Wives Club, a local YWCA organization, was actively serving "war brides" brought to Terre Haute by husbands who had served overseas. By the winter of 1945, millions of American military personnel from all over the globe were returning home. In addition, sixty thousand wives and sweethearts hoped to join their significant others in the United States. However, these women were not allowed to immigrate at that time because of the Immigration Act of 1924. Pressure from various sources caused the United States Congress to pass the War Brides Act of 1945.

The following brief anecdote gives insight into Terre Haute YWCA's role in assisting young women who immigrated to the United States as recent brides (and brides-to-be) of WWII military personnel. At the age of ninety-five, Mrs. Edward (Muriel) Allen related her experiences during an interview in the summer of 2021.

Muriel Allen

Muriel was a seventeen-year-old living in England when she met her husband-to-be, Edward, during special events sponsored by her church. A short time later, "her soldier" was shipped home to the United States. By this time, they had formed definite plans, which had her joining him in Terre Haute. After the war in Europe, Edward was able to arrange a seventeen-hour flight from France to Indianapolis and on to Terre Haute. After settling in, Muriel saw a newspaper article announcing the monthly meeting of a group of war brides at the YWCA. It was a support group helping with solutions for childcare and other issues; working to resolve language barriers was a common objective. According to Muriel, Ernestine McDougal, executive director at the time, was "treasured" for all the assistance the YWCA offered. Muriel and Edward were married in 1946 and were together until his death in 2000.

Overseas Wives Club

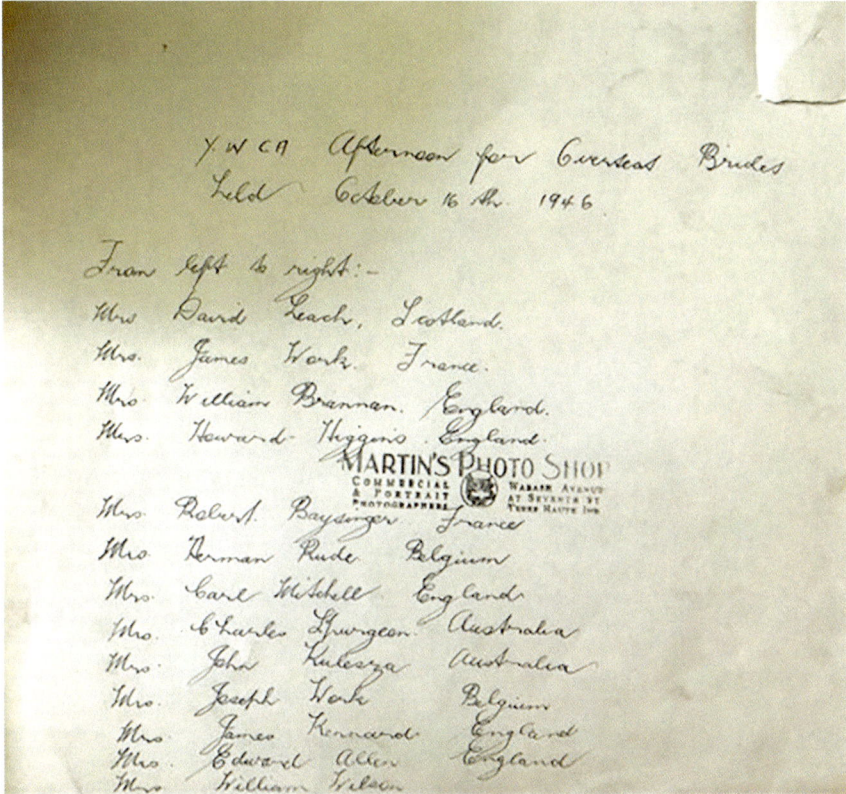

War Brides List
Muriel 2nd from bottom

Blue Triangle Becomes Y-Teens

The Girl Reserve and Blue Triangle organizations were renamed in 1947 as the "Y-Teen Clubs." (That organization was renamed again in 1992 as "YW Teens.") Y-Teens Clubs continued encouraging teens to become active community leaders as adults. Activities focused on team building, leadership skills, special event planning, business skills, communication skills, and just having fun. A common memory of many members was the Harvest Moon Dance and the February Sweetheart Dance, the first formal dance for many. For several years, the Terre Haute YWCA had more teenage members than any other YWCA in Indiana.

YW Teens

It is time to sign-up for YW-Teens. This year the club will be doing many exciting activities. We will do many community service projects, learn leadership skills, and plan many community events. The YW-Teens will be involved with traditional events (the dances) and many new events. Come be a part of Decision 2001. Decision 2001 will plan events for teens in the Wabash Valley. The possibilities are limitless. Attend the YW-Teen kick-off meeting on Monday, September 10, 2001. You can make your voice heard in the Wabash Valley as a leader in the community.

YW Teens

Harvest Moon Dance

Y Teens Group

Related Materials

Blue Triangle Ball attendees
Oct 1929

Blue Triangle Girls demonstrating
1943 styles

INDIANA

TENTH ANNUAL REPORT

of the

Young Women's Christian Association

TERRE HAUTE, INDIANA
121 NORTH SEVENTH STREET
Citizens Phone 1353, Bell Phone 2191

YEAR ENDING APRIL 30, 1912

Purpose: The Spiritual, Intellectual, Social and Physical
Development of Women

Organized 1902. Incorporated May 30, 1904

Affiliated with National Board of Young Women's Christian
Association of America

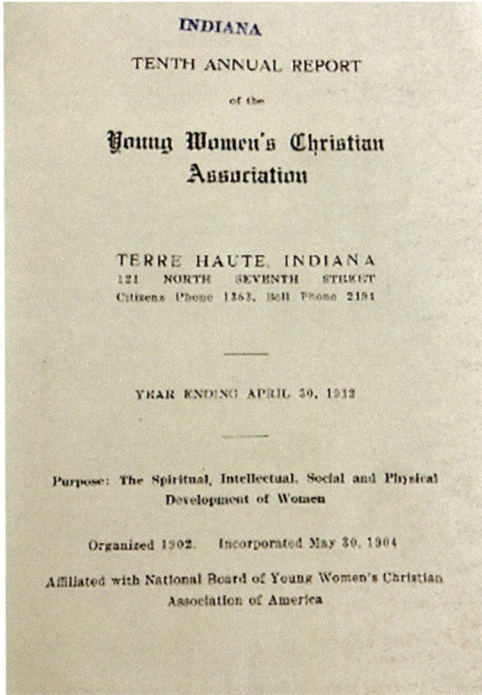

10th Annual Report

Membership

Any woman of good moral character may become a member of the Young Women's Christian Association.

FEES

Regular Members.............$1.00 per year
Sustaining Members............ 5.00 per year
Junior Members............... .50 per year

Life Members—$100 given at one time.
The present membership is 612; of this number 517 are regular, 33 sustaining, 50 juniors, 12 life.

The Young Women's Christian Association

FOR THE YEAR 1909

RELIGIOUS WORK DEPARTMENT

Vesper Hour. Noon Meetings. Bible Classes: Morning, Afternoon and Evening.
FREE TO ALL.

EDUCATIONAL DEPARTMENT

Domestic Science, Correct Serving, Theory and Practice.

DOMESTIC ARTS

Millinery, Sewing, Embroidery. Will open October 1, 1909.

PHYSICAL TRAINING

Gymnasium, Floor Work, Basket-ball, Swimming.

Classes will be formed in other branches when there is a demand for them.

GYMNASIUM

Director, Miss Edna Price Brown, New Haven Normal School of Gymnastics, 1905.

Classes will begin Jan. 11. Term, 28 lessons. Classes meeting twice a week.

10th Annual Report Inner Page

Chapter 3 The Post-War YWCA
The 1940s and 1950s

Advancing Diversity in Terre Haute

The YWCA was a pioneer in the Terre Haute community in promoting racial integration. Two African-American women were elected to the board of directors in 1948. Shortly after, the YW's food service was opened to African-Americans. In 1952 the pool was integrated. These moves, in a still segregated community, took courage from the YWCA women. Other groups in the community joined in support of the YW's leadership. In February 1949, Rabbi Leonard J. Mervis spoke to the YWCA on the fight against prejudice. He gave examples of other communities where progress toward integration had been made. He emphasized that education, religion, and law were positive forces for brotherhood.

Expanding Demographics Served

At the 46th annual membership meeting of the YWCA, Mrs. Boyd I. Miller of Indianapolis summarized how the YWCAs had grown to include a membership of both women and girls and services for teens, business and professional women, homemakers, and students. In addition to membership benefits, safe living quarters were available for young working women, as well as job training and social and recreational facilities. The 1940s ended with local membership approaching 1,000; Y-Teens membership in seventeen county schools totaled 1,700 young girls. One hundred thirty girls lived in the residence during the year, with twenty-five residing for the entire year. Other examples of YW offerings included: The Business and Professional League with Kathleen Smith as president with a membership of twenty-three meetings twice monthly. Overseas Wives with Mrs. Theodore Palmer met regularly with a membership of thirteen war brides.

Shortly after the YWCA's initial steps toward integration, a group of African-American women members of the Business and Professional Women's Club organized The Y's Urbans. A review of Terre Haute newspapers shows regular monthly meetings through 1977.

YWCA's Y's Urbans

Club 121

Club 121 opened on December 22, 1945, for young people between eighteen and thirty-five. It was sponsored by volunteers headed by Miss Hazel Cadden as chair of the committee. Membership was open to men and women for recreation, dancing, games, swimming, and special entertainment. In addition to dances and parties, a wide range of classes was offered, from swimming and health education to public speaking and sewing. Meetings were scheduled on Friday, Saturday, and Sunday evenings from 8:30 until 11:30. As of August 1946, the *Saturday Spectator* reported that "250 to 300 young persons have visited the club in the past month." It was an outgrowth of the USO Sycamore Center, which had occupied the YWCA's social lounges and recreation rooms. Charter members were Junior USO Hostesses, residence women of the YWCA, and members of Beta Chi, the younger business girls' sorority. Later, membership was extended to students at Indiana State Teachers College, Rose Polytechnic Institute, and local business schools. The Club operated through the early 1950s.

Club 121 Members

On the 50th anniversary of the Association's founding, membership included nearly 1,200 junior and senior high school girls in Y-Teens Clubs, and 250 young women were participating in the Association's business girl groups. Health education covered the age span from preschool to adult. The residence continued to serve students and young working women. At the celebration, this YWCA philosophy concerning young women and girls was noted: "the belief in the right of every individual to be herself, respect for the dignity of each personality, and the assurance of fellowship with others working together for the common good."

The Golden Age Club

The Golden Age Club was organized at the YWCA in the fall of 1952 by Mrs. Caribelle Dickey, Mrs. Blanche Wolf, Mrs. Elizabeth Nattkemper, and Miss Laura Shryer with financial aid from the Altrusa Club. A new idea in Terre Haute was a counterpart of older people's clubs in other sections of the nation, particularly in Florida and California. For the ensuing twenty-five years, weekly meetings were held with multiple programs of interest to those over age 50. Average membership, open to both men and women, ranged from 60 to over 100 persons. The Club was known for bringing together seniors; a few couples married as a result of meeting at the Club.

Golden Age Club Meeting

Married after joining GAC

1968 Golden Age Club Officers

Food Services Changes

The *Terre Haute Tribune* released news on September 6, 1958, that the YWCA was changing hours. The cafeteria would re-open with new hours, Monday through Friday, 11:00 a.m. until 2:00 p.m. As always, men and women were welcomed, and banquets were available by appointment. This announcement was followed by discouraging news less than a year later. Ernestine McDougal, executive director, announced that on Friday, June 12, 1959, noon food service would close.

YWCA.

YWCA WILL CLOSE NOON FOOD SERVICE

The YWCA noon food service will close Friday, June 12, it was announced today by Mrs. Ernestine McDougal, executive secretary of the Y.

Catering service will be available for special groups upon request, she stated. For information on this service call the YWCA.

Food Service Closes

Supporting Fitness

The YW's continued interest in health issues led to the opening of a health salon in May 1959. The announcement described the additional equipment as "ten different units which afford a massage to the spine, back, waist, hips, thighs, and arms. Two gyro belts and other miscellaneous devices . . . ensure figure control, muscle tone, and improved posture."

Terre Haute YWCA
Organization at Time of 50th Anniversary

1952 Board Members

Mrs. Clyde Andrews	Mrs. W. N. McCutchan
Mrs. Cloyd Anthony	Mrs. Skander Newport
Mrs. Clyde Bryant	Miss Juliet Peddle
Mrs. Fred Brengle	Mrs. J.H. Petty
Mrs. Charlotte Burford	Mrs. Rutherford Porter
Mrs. Samuel Carruth	Mrs. Fred Powell
Mrs. Edward Chaskin	Mrs. Homer Powell
Mrs. E. Lee Davis	Mrs. James Richart
Mrs. T. H. Dix	Mrs. Mary Hill Sankey
Mrs. Elmer Douglas	Mrs. Marvin Shelton
Mrs. A. Stanley Dreyfus	Miss Mary Lou Sherer
Mrs. Harvey Froderman	Mrs. John Thompson
Mrs. Richard Gemmecke	Mrs. Hazel Dodge Turman
Mrs. Pearl York Gibson	Mrs. Wayne Weber
Mrs. L. A. Malone	

Trustees

Staff

Chapter 4 Dealing with Disaster
The 1960s

Changes in Leadership

The resignation of Ernestine McDougal was effective at the end of the contract year on August 31, 1960. She had served as executive director, beginning in 1948, after teaching YWCA classes, directing adult activities, and serving on the board of directors. On June 22, 1960, the *Terre Haute Tribune* announced the appointment of Elizabeth Nattkemper as executive director. Mrs. Nattkemper had served for seven years as director of health, physical education, and recreation.

Elizabeth Nattkemper

Major Contribution

February 1960 witnessed another major announcement; a significant financial contribution to the YWCA. Mrs. Quinn McBeth, board president, announced that $132,000 had been received from the estate of Fannie R. Foster. Mrs. McBeth indicated that $110,000 had been invested and placed in the Foster Building Fund, $17,000 had been deposited in local building and loan associations, and $5,000 was placed in the YWCA capital fund. Mrs. McBeth added that the building fund would be used to modernize the present building or form the nucleus of a fund for a new building.

Disaster Strikes - Custodian Killed

The decade of the 1950s ended with the association successfully providing a wide assortment of services and sponsoring special interest groups. It was expected that the next decade would follow in kind. That expectation suffered a setback on Tuesday morning, September 19, 1961. Several theories were advanced, with the FBI and local officials concluding that a horrible accident had struck the YWCA building killing the custodian, 63-year-old Carl Ross.

Girls in Street after Explosion

Residents reported that Ross had yelled warnings telling them to exit the building via the "back way." Some fled using the fire escape. Even though the blast occurred before the residents could leave the building, no one was injured. Apparently, the explosion was located on the lower level, and in the early morning hours, the residents were in their rooms on the second and third floors. Due to international tensions of the era, several young women were interviewed as they waited in the street. One woman said, "I thought the Russians had bombed us." Interestingly, a Red Cross Nursing Workshop had been scheduled on that day entitled "The Work of a Nurse in Time of Disaster." It was rescheduled for the following evening in a different room.

After several months of investigation, a consensus of theories was published in the *Terre Haute Tribune* on February 15, 1962. The essence of that article is as follows.

"The explosion at the YWCA . . . may have been caused by decomposed dynamite left over from stocks of a firm in the neighborhood which handled the explosive during World War II, according to Chief of Police Frank Riddle. However, Chief Riddle has emphasized that it was only a theory and that officers were still investigating the blast that claimed Ross's life.

Ross was killed by the explosion, which occurred seconds after he shouted a warning to the women residents of the YWCA during the early morning hours. Police theorized that he found the explosive in the boiler room and was rushing it outside when it exploded. A revised theory stated that Ross could have found the old dynamite and was taking it to the basement of the building when it exploded. Riddle added that decomposed dynamite becomes 'very critical' and could be touched off by jarring it. Through all the police leads, no definite motive for either suicide or murder has been established."

None of the investigations discovered metal particles or other materials that might be used to build a bomb. Officials agreed that Ross would have quickly recognized several sticks of dynamite. They concluded that the victim was "desperately attempting to remove some article from the building when the matter suddenly let go cutting Ross down in his tracks."

Carl Ross

Carl Ross' obituary described the victim of the blast as primarily a churchman. He was a trustee of the Church of Christ, at Twenty-first and Elm Streets, for five years. His brother, Jimmy, who had worked for years across the street from the YW at the Elks Club, mentioned that Carl worked in the mines as a mule driver twenty years or so earlier, Carl had lived in Vigo County all his life, having been born and reared in the Lost Creek community. Survivors included his wife, Marie; two daughters; three stepsons; and other relatives including twelve grandchildren and one great-grandchild.

Eight weeks after the explosion, Mrs. Margaret Wright, director of health, physical education and recreation, announced the pool would reopen. All classes were to resume as originally scheduled. The September blast that took the life of the building's janitor damaged the building, particularly the area around and near the pool. The following review of the repairs was written for the *Terre Haute Tribune.*

> "**The pool area has been completely remodeled, including lowered ceilings of acoustical tile. The color scheme is turquoise and white. Incorporated in the remodeling is a new downstairs lounge which will be open for use by swimmers, parents and friends about the first of the year. All rooms in the downstairs area have been newly plastered and the final decorating will be done during the Christmas holiday season.**
>
> **The large dressing room and its showers are ready for use when classes start on Thursday. Included in the swimming schedule is the new 'swim and stay fit' program of the American Red Cross, which grants special cards for swimming participants for ten, twenty and up to fifty miles. The 50-mile swimmers receive a gold 50-mile club card. Several YW swimmers were expected to earn this card before the start of the summer swimming season.**"

The pool and the programs consistently ranked among the most popular activities at the YW. In June 1962, the YW announced that 200 fourth, fifth, and sixth-grade girls registered for YWCA's "Learn to Swim Week." A total of fifty girls earned perfect attendance marks, with thirty girls earning Red Cross beginner swim cards.

As part of their effort to help improve the health and physical well-being of the women of Terre Haute, the YWCA purchased a new Sauna Bath for the use of its members. The announcement of the purchase added that "science has found no substitute for the benefits to be had from the application of controlled moist heat that completely circulates about the body. Originated by the Egyptians, popularized by the Romans, and improved by the Finns, sauna baths are gaining popularity in America."

Brotherhood

In late 1963, Mrs. Jean Lehman, resident director of the Terre Haute YWCA (and was present the night of the explosion), wrote an article on "brotherhood," which was subsequently published in the YWCA Magazine for December. In the article, Mrs. Lehman wrote that at the time, the word "brotherhood" was often given lip service. Still, she questioned whether many people would meet the test of living "under the same roof with persons of another race, color, or religion."

Mrs. Lehman wrote that at the YWCA, she had seen the true meaning of brotherhood (of sisterhood). She pointed out "that at the YWCA, there were Oriental, Negro, and Caucasian races. We have girls of the Catholic, Protestant, Greek Orthodox, Jewish, Moslem, and Buddhist faiths."

Mrs. Lehman stated that "these girls make it seem easy; they seem to melt into a pattern of brotherhood living. It never occurs to them that they are doing or living any differently. Each accepts the other as an equal. They have no bylaws, rules of literature, or even suggestions of how to get along. They just live together, learning each other's ways, sharing their problems, clothes, food, and most of all, their friendship and love."

She summarized: "I have heard people say it can't be done – this true living of brotherhood. It can be done, I see it every day, week, month, and year. After five years as residence director in a Young Women's Christian Association, I can truly say, 'It can be done.'"

Commemoration of United Nations

The YWCA took every opportunity to promote understanding among individuals of differing backgrounds. This was evident at a tree planting on the campus of Indiana State College in 1963. The ceremony was to commemorate the twentieth anniversary of the founding of the United Nations. Individuals participating represented Iran, Hong Kong, Nigeria, Turkey, and South Vietnam with officials of the YWCA and Indiana State College.

Tree Planting Ceremony

Related Materials

1968 Board of Directors

Four Generations of Swimmers

Chapter 5 Bursting at the Seams
The 1970s

Matineers

In September 1970, a group within the YWCA organized to provide another valued service to members. Named the "40 Matineers," or often just "Matineers," the group operated under the leadership of Ruth Melloh, program director at the YWCA. The group's first tours included seeing theater productions at Clowes Hall in Indianapolis. These trips were supported by people unable to attend evening performances at the theater. Similar tour groups were common in many communities during the seventies.

Matineers

The schedules called for the bus to stop at several convenient locations: First, the YWCA, then Meadows Shopping Center, and finally, the I-70 and Highway 59 interchange near Brazil, Indiana. Lunch was scheduled in Indianapolis, followed by the production at Clowes Hall.

The club was open to men and women members of the YWCA. In 1973, tour participation had grown to include 80 members and required two busses for trips to Indianapolis. Tour destinations were added as varied interests were expressed. Special trips were scheduled to areas of interest around the Midwest, including Brown County to see the Fall colors, Columbus, Indiana, to appreciate its architecture, and Chicago and St. Louis to experience other cultural attractions.

Building Community

The early seventies witnessed an effort of the YWCA to work with varied groups "around town" to build a more cohesive and understanding community. Tours of Terre Haute churches was one such effort. The first annual church tour was held on March 31, 1970. Churches participating in the morning tour were: First Baptist, Seventh Day Adventist, Trinity Lutheran, and Greek Orthodox. The afternoon session included: St. Mary-of-the-Woods Chapels, Maple Avenue Methodist, and the Hebrew Synagogue.

Church Tour Group

In a continuing effort to expand community understanding, "Days at the Y" were offered. These events for adult members featured a morning program, and a luncheon, followed by an afternoon program to unite women of various ages, races, and/or income levels in an informal and comfortable environment. A prime example of a typical program was presented in January 1977 and hosted by the Armchair Travelers Club of the YWCA. The program included a morning slide show presented by Valda Kester, who spent four years in India while her husband participated in a U.S. Aid agricultural project. The afternoon program featured singing and dancing by Nasrat Sultana Aslam, a radio performer in India, before becoming a citizen of Pakistan. She moved to Terre Haute to be with her husband studying electronics at Indiana State University.

Aslam's performance at the Armchair Travelers Club of the YWCA's program was followed by Mrs. Veno Rathee, who discussed life and customs in India. Mrs. Rathee grew up in India and in 1977 became an employee of the Vigo County Welfare Department in 1977.

Day at the Y

**Mrs. Venu Rathee and Mrs Valda Kester
Sharing Indian Culture**

Need Growing for New Facility

For the YWCA, the 1970s were a period of transition. To say that since the YWCA's beginning, the culture had evolved and the attitudes toward women had changed would be a major understatement. Women were no longer considered incapable of taking care of themselves. Housing for single women had become an option, multiple and varied restaurants, including fast food stops, such as McDonald's, had begun to populate the area, and opportunities for a wide variety of social interactions were easily accessed. The consequences of this transition directly impacted the YWCA, its programs, service activities, and building and staffing needs.

1975 Officers: Mrs. Fred Kramer, Treas; Mrs. Robert Puckett, 2nd VP; Mrs. Frank Schoaff, Sec.; Mrs James Martin, 1st VP; Mrs Robert Peterson, Pres.

During the 1970s, the YWCA's leaders began to recognize the need to expand the available space and improve the equipment. In addition, as nearby public parking lots closed, there was only one solution: a fund drive for a new building – only the second YWCA fund drive ever conducted in Terre Haute.

At the annual meeting of the YWCA board of directors, it was announced that committees had been meeting and the administrators were planning on vacating the present building on 7th Street. At that time, the board was exploring the acquisition of a portion of the recently vacated Wiley High School property. During the same timeframe, the annual report showed 407 YWCA groups had conducted 3,188 sessions with an enrollment of 6,495 participants. Clearly, the YW was a viable organization requiring an appropriate facility.

Expanding Programs for Community's Youth

In the meantime, the YW continued to expand its services to the community by pursuing new approaches. Those efforts included cooperative sponsorships between the YWCA and other organizations with similar interests. One of those ventures was with the Cooperative Extension Office to provide preschool information to young mothers.

Cooperative extension mothers

Not all of the YWCA's outreach programs were successful. In late 1969, young women students at Indiana State University were contacted by Mrs. Nattkemper to organize a student YWCA patterned after Y-Teen Clubs in high schools. There was an element of caution to the announcement because approximately 30 members had committed to memberships, but more would be needed. In addition, an earlier student chapter at ISU had dissolved. A newspaper report indicated that the chapter was active in 1972 but soon dissolved. In the fall of 1970, the YWCA named a program director for junior high school and college activities at the YWCA. Dorothy Jerse would guide those programs until 1974.

**Dorothy Jerse with
Indiana State University student**

New Youth Directors Announced

Ruby Daniels was named Young People's Program Director in late 1975 to direct Kiddy Kampers, Junior Janes, and Live Yer events. In December 1977, Patricia Buckner was named Youth Director responsible for those programs and other organized activities for older Y Teen girl members in junior and senior high schools.

Eva Hopp and Ruby Daniels

Patricia Buckner

Throughout the seventies, programs were established by Mrs. Jerse to concentrate on the needs of girls in early grades. For an example, Junior Janes was a girls' group for ages K through third grade. Eight-week classes, "Fun Saturdays," and special one-week summer sessions included crafts, cooking, and swimming were among other programs offered. Gail Hayes, who became teen program director in 1988, was a member of the 1972 Junior Janes shown in the included picture. She remembered activities at the YW, field trips, and swimming in the pool, "which smelled of very strong chlorine."

Junior Janes

Swimming programs were always among the most popular offered at the YWCA. They were especially popular and well attended with the young, including the Rankin Headstart children.

Head Start Swimmers

Considering Broader Issues

In the early months of 1971, an eight-week discussion series was announced to "provide an opportunity for persons to learn, discuss, and speak out on eight critical foreign policy issues facing the United States. Topics included "Vietnam, Laos, and Cambodia: Which Way to Peace and When?" and "The Middle East Conflict: Is Peaceful Settlement Possible?"

Issues of race had been an area of focus for the YWCA for decades but were becoming more important in the seventies. An example of efforts to address the issue was held in the fall of 1971. "Interaction – Black and White" was the theme of an all-day meeting at the Terre

Haute YWCA. Mrs. Geraldine Bradford, commissioner and delegate to the Indiana Civil Rights Commission, rendered leadership to the meeting. At the time, she was serving her second term as president of the YWCA Board.

Geraldine Bradford

Planning for a New Building

The demands for a facility to accommodate the growing needs of the YW kept the focus on the replacement of the North Seventh Street building. The first site considered for the new YWCA was at Poplar and Seventh Streets, the vacated location of Wiley High School. In June 1971, the Vigo County Public Library Board of Trustees heard a request from the YWCA for a price on a parcel of land at the new library location. The Vigo County Library Board had acquired the property for a new building, and they determined that there was insufficient space for both the library and the YWCA with parking for both. Later, land in Fairbanks Park on the banks of the Wabash River, which the Girl Scouts were leasing, became available.

In early January 1973, Terre Haute Mayor William J. Brighton announced at a press conference that the Park Board, with the cooperation of the Covered Bridge Girl Scout Council, had authorized the YWCA to share their lease on 6.2 acres at Fairbanks Park.

Later in January, Mrs. Eva Hopp, president of the YWCA Board of Directors, shared sketches and details of the proposed building with the public. The initial planning by the architect, Ewing Miller, showed a two-level building with ground-level entrances to both levels. It was to have a large multi-purpose room with smaller rooms and club rooms nearby. A large kitchen was planned along with a large pool area and a modern locker and shower complex. Adjacent to the pool and at the same level was a smaller multipurpose room for physical education, small meeting rooms, offices for staff, and a reception lounge to complete the facility. It had been designed to meet the "total needs of the YWCA in its service to women, girls, and families of Terre Haute and the Wabash Valley. It was noted that there were no plans to include a residential component since the national trend was for YWCAs to discontinue housing facilities.

A few days later, the *Terre Haute Tribune* announced a campaign goal of $750,000 for a new facility. The estimated cost of the building was $900,000, which included proceeds from the sale of the Seventh Street facility. Don Pendergast served as general chairman of the fund drive. At the same time, Terre Haute advertising executive Arnold DeRolf was named Public Relations Chairman of the YWCA Developments Capital Funds Campaign. Commercial Solvent Corporation presented the first major industrial gift of $10,000 in February 1973.

Mrs. Eva Hopp became the executive director of the YWCA in July 1973. Her predecessor, Mrs. Elizabeth Nattkemper, had served for thirteen years in that capacity.

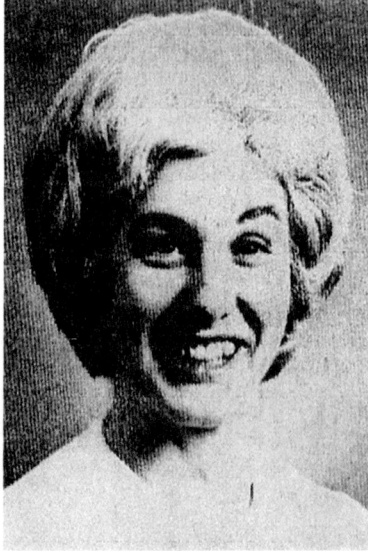

Eva Hopp

The fundraising drive continued through January 1975, when Don Pendergast decided to complete and close the drive. Approximately $300,000 of the $400,000 needed for the facility was raised through the campaign. Because the building fund had fallen short of the initial goal, building plans were downsized. In June 1975, a builder, Marsh, Inc. (Hannig and Associates), was announced. Construction was to begin in late summer, with completion expected approximately twelve months later.

On September 13, 1975, "For Sale" signs were posted in the windows of the YWCA building at 121 North Seventh Street. First opened in 1908, the building was one of the city's landmarks in the downtown area.

> YWCA—121 N. 7th St. — 3-story brick building. First floor consists of lounge rooms, meeting rooms and offices. Second floor, 5 resident rooms, kitchen and laundry facilities. Third floor, 20 sleeping rooms. Throughout the building there are ample toilet facilities. There is a swimming pool. Building is heated by stoker fire boiler.

Building for Sale

In October, a sublease was approved with the Girls Scouts and by the Terre Haute Park Board. By November 1975, the YWCA Board had approved the building plans and authorized the contractor to begin work. A groundbreaking ceremony was scheduled for mid-December. The estimated cost was $418,251 and did not include pool or site work costs. The sale of the Seventh Street building was expected to bring the total available funds to approximately $400,000.

Groundbreaking – December 19, 1975

A description of the groundbreaking was published in the *Terre Haute Tribune* on Friday, December 19, 1975.

> **"Braving a wind chill of more than ten degrees below zero, some 100 persons turned out Thursday afternoon for the ground-breaking ceremonies of the new $400,000 YWCA building at Fairbanks Park. The group, bundled in heavy overcoats, scarfs, gloves, and earmuffs, included the following: Mrs. Eva Hopp, executive director of the YWCA; Marion Underwood, president of the YWCA trustee board; Don Pendergast, building ad fund chairman; sister Jean Fuqua, president of the Covered Bridge Council; Shelton Hannig, builder; Ed Howard,**

president of the United Way; Mrs. Geraldine Bradford, former president of the YWCA board; Mrs. Elizabeth Nattkemper, former executive director of the YWCA; Fred Ruby, co-chairman of the fund drive; the Rev. John Chironna; Arnold DeRolf, committee member; and Mrs. Arnes Peterson, president of the YWCA board of directors."

The final plan for the exterior of the building was to be 127 feet by 82 feet (10,400+ square feet) with exterior walls of red cedar batten and face brick. The interior would include a large multipurpose room, offices, an exercise-dance area, a children's room, a lounge and reception room, a vending area, a mechanical room, and storage areas. Two seminar rooms were planned for class and workshop use and could be combined into one large room when needed. A lack of funds forced the YWCA to postpone the construction of a pool, additional dressing rooms, and additional storage until phase II could be implemented.

In March 1976, it was announced that Charles Evinger, a local developer, had purchased the North Seventh Street building for $45,000. Evinger mentioned several proposed uses for the facility, including student rentals. The building would continue to provide housing for residents until June 15, 1976, a date marking the end of school terms at Indiana State University and Indiana Vocational Technical College.

The period from August 23 through September was set aside for moving, with activities restarting at the new location after September 7, 1976.

The end of an era and the end of one of the YWCA's original purposes was signaled by a photograph in the *Terre Haute Tribune* on Monday, August 16, 1976. The last residents of the YWCA were pictured leaving the building for the final time. The local YWCA was founded in 1902 to provide safe "room and board" for young working women. That function was no longer needed.

Residents leaving YWCA at 121 N. 7th Street

Air National Guard helps move to Fairbanks Park YWCA

A Grand Opening

On Sunday, October 24, 1976, a public dedication of the new YWCA building was held. Several dignitaries spoke at the afternoon ceremony. Dedication activities extended through the week of October 25 and ended with informal building tours on Saturday, October 30, with the Harvest Moon Ball scheduled for that evening at Indiana State University.

It was announced at the dedication that the public auction of the furnishings at the former building had raised $7,000, and contributions from the community had provided funds to permit the purchase of furnishings for the child care rooms, the quiet lounge, the kitchen, and seminar rooms.

YWCA at Fairbanks Park

Two features that were postponed in the original construction were the pool and landscaping. In 1977 the exterior of the building and the surrounding site received attention from volunteers, including the Kiwanis Club, High School Key Clubs, and Circle K Club of Indiana State University. These groups worked to blend the building with the natural landscape of the riverbank. Bunch Nurseries assisted in the design and contributed landscape materials.

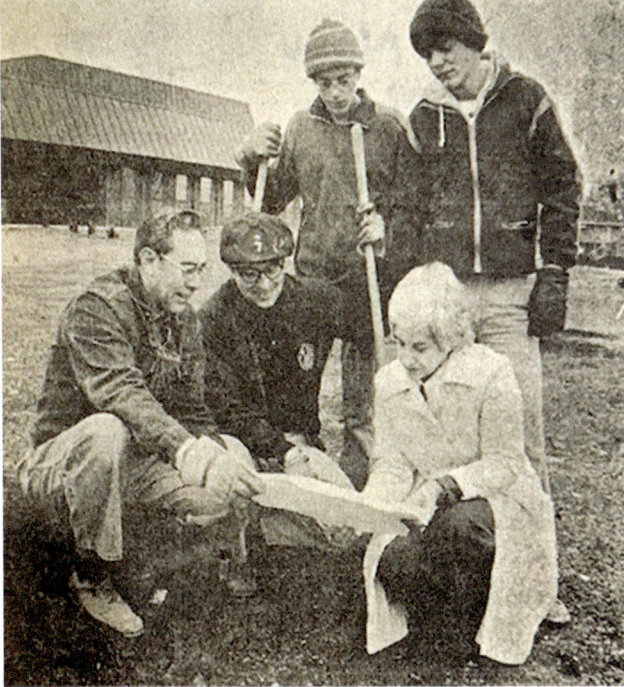

Landscaping 1977

Although the YWCA had been in the Fairbanks Building for a short time, preliminary architectural plans for a swimming pool had been completed. A dinner dance was held in May 1977, with proceeds from the event to be earmarked for the "new $300,000 pool."

More Multifaceted Programs

Programs offered and planned continued to expand in breadth and variety. In addition to the "usual" YWCA offerings, "Practical Parent" programs delving into areas of child abuse, divorce, marriage, and family life improvement were added. In addition, classes for the developmentally disabled and programs on alcoholism, stress, tension, and homemaking skills were offered. A small sample of future programs included: metric system training, programs on legal rights of teens and adults, consumer needs, racism sensitivity, and others to increase awareness of women's community contributions.

The local Y-Me Breast Cancer Chapter provided information, emotional support, and coping mechanisms and held monthly meetings for the community. The YWCA established a "Working Woman's Clothes Closet." The "Closet" provided one appropriate outfit suitable for an interview, followed by two outfits if hired.

In May 1977, the Girls Club of Terre Haute honored Mrs. Dorothy Jerse as "Woman of the Year" during its second annual awards dinner. Mrs. Jerse had already built an impressive resume of contributions to the YWCA, especially notable in the areas of youth programs, having initiated three new age-group activities. The community would soon see her contributions to the YWCA become even more impressive.

On June 21, 1977, the YWCA had a Diamond Jubilee luncheon to celebrate the 75th anniversary of the YWCA in Terre Haute. Mrs. Dorothy Clark, a well-known local historian, spoke on the rich history of the local YWCA and its impact on the community.

The 1970s ended with a membership of nearly 2,000, according to Mrs. Gordon Hulman, president of the Board of Directors. She added that the "YWCA is the world's oldest and largest multi-racial women's membership organization working toward the elimination of racism and sexism so that all women can realize their contribution to their community, the nation, and the world." The local YWCA scheduled its meeting of Interracial Families on Saturday, January 7, 1978. A carry-in dessert was planned with films and discussion topics for parents.

The YWCA continued a diverse offering of activities in '78 and '79. The following is a small sample: "The YWCA is offering an early summer trip to Austria, the beautiful land of 'The Sound of Music'; "The American Heart Association will be conducting a CPR Workshop"; "YWCA and Public Service to offer microwave oven class"; Chicago trip planned to shop, visit a museum, or see a show in the Windy City"; YWCA brings an outdoor circus to Terre Haute with the world's largest round tent"; and the Second Annual YWCA Benefit Dinner and Dance was scheduled for June.

In August 1978, Eva Hopp, executive director, and her assistant director, Janice Oblak, resigned. Karen Davies served as executive director for five years until 1983.

On July 30, 1979, Indiana State University announced that demolition would soon begin on the east side of Seventh Street and include the YWCA building.

Related Materials

**Architects' plan
For Fairbanks Park YWCA**

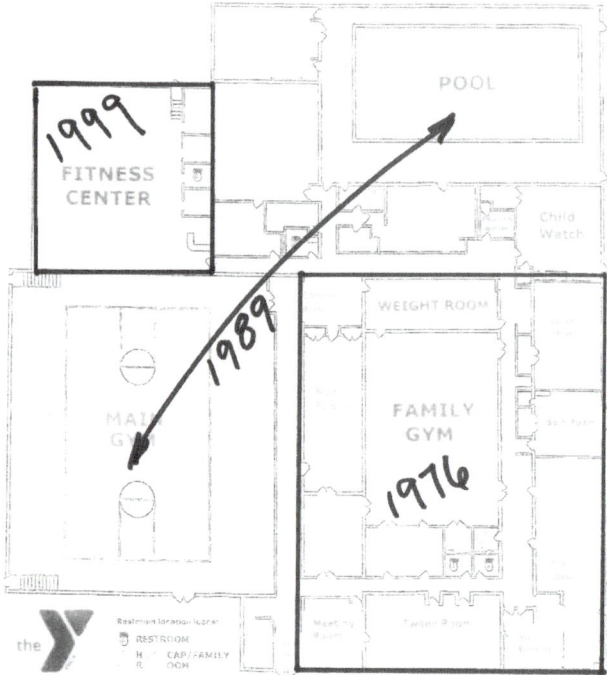

**Floor Plan
Original 1976 + 1989 Expansion + 1999 Addition**

Dr. Hopp with Junior Janes

Chapter 6 Programs, Programs, and Expansion
The 1980s

Dancing at the YWCA

In the early 1900s, the residents of Terre Haute were similar to residents of other growing industrial centers. They were often described as "working hard and playing hard." A common feature of the entertainment industry was an abundance of dance halls. Many considered these as sordid places leading women into an immoral life.

When the YWCA was originally organized in 1902 - and for a few years after - dancing was considered, at a minimum, inappropriate for a proper young woman and YWCA member. In June 1913, the *Saturday Spectator* published an article commenting on the change in public attitudes.

"Nothing more strikingly accentuates the change in Young Women's Christian Association work than its attitude toward dancing. Only a few years back, the idea of allowing dancing to be taught at a YWCA would have been regarded as joining with the emissaries of the devil. Now every director of physical training must be an accomplished instructor in dancing.

Dancing is now generally recognized as promoting good manners and as a means of keeping the body in good form while cultivating grace of movement and good carriage. The old, boisterous forfeit kissing games have been discarded for the more refined dancing as a health giving and pleasurable mode of diversion. It is true that there is indecent dancing, but refined people are not guilty of such offense any more than they are of using vulgar language."

Later, in October 1920, the *Saturday Spectator* reported that after the war, YWCA girls considered dances an "absolute necessity" as much as the comforts of home the YW offered. Mrs. Winnifred Taylor, general secretary, commented, "We've been very successful with our dances. The girls enjoyed them so much, and the young men who have the privilege of attending – upon invitation of the young women, of course – tell us repeatedly that the YW is so much different than what they thought it was. We've been having one dance a month for the girls."

Dance Class

In addition to social dancing, organized instruction in dance began soon after the YWCA occupied the new building at North Seventh Street. Miss Eunice Ruth Augur came to the YW in 1909 as the head of the physical training and hygiene department. In 1911, an article in the *Saturday Spectator* described her approach as follows: "She does not confine her instruction merely to calisthenic exercises, but gives a running lecture on hygiene, the care of the body, the use of specific exercises to correct . . . She has introduced aesthetic dances, calculated not alone to develop muscles and brain, as their prime motives, but simply to make the individual graceful, to enable her to fully enjoy the poetry of rhythmic motion." The article continued, "When dancing steps were introduced, one mother made a complaint by saying: 'I did not send my daughter to learn to dance.' This season the mother has joined the class herself."

In 1911, eighty-two Wiley high school girls enrolled in Miss Augur's classes with fees paid by the school board.

Kicking Up Heels

A continuous succession of YWCA instructors provided a variety of instruction in dance from the beginning of the YW until the current generation. Two instructors that served for extended careers were Roseann Callahan and Marge Stahley.

Stahley continues dancing tradition

YWCA

Terre Haute has always been known as a good "dance town" with parents interested in enriching their children's lives through dance classes. The YWCA has been a part of this local dance scene for many years.

There are probably a thousand or more persons in the Wabash Valley now who remember studying dance under Rose Ann Callahan, YWCA dance instructor from 1952 to 1976.

The dance program continues at the YWCA with this tradition under Marge Stahley's leadership. Stahley began her study of dance at the age of three years. Her training in ballet, tap and jazz includes study under Mary Helen Murphy, Lynette Schlale and dance faculty at Butler University. She continues to participate in workshops to gain new ideas, saying, "a good dance teacher has to keep up or she falls behind in every way."

Stahley moved to Terre Haute four years ago when her husband, Wayne, was appointed head football coach at North Vigo High School. She came with 10 years teaching experience at Southside Dance Studio and Linda Leonard's in Indianapolis and at N.A.D.A.A. workshops.

The dance program at the YWCA is more than weekly classes. Stahley says, "I like to keep our students involved in as many dance

activities as possible. We went to Dance Caravan in Cincinnati this summer to study under the Broadway dancers and choreographers. Two of our "troupe classes" also competed in the Showcase Talent Contest, Indianapolis, bringing home first and third place awards.

Locally, the YWCA danced down Ohio Boulevard last month as part of this annual YWCA-Meis event and two of our dancers took second place award at the recent Terre Haute Park Department Talent Show. In addition YWCA dancers will be at Honey Creek Square to demonstrate our skills at 1:30 p.m. Sunday.

YWCA dance classes are scheduled by age and skill grouping during late afternoon and evening hours Monday through Thursday. Classes meet once weekly through the school year and are available for persons three years old through teen and adult age. Fees are $1.75 and $2.50 per class. Persons interested in this dance program may telephone 232-3358 or stop by the YWCA in Fairbanks Park for additional details.

Stahley and Callahan – YW Dance Instructors

Dance Group

Dancing Down the Boulevard

Women Unlimited

The Women Unlimited Committee of the YWCA held a series of benefit dinner dances, known as "International Interlude," beginning in 1977. Proceeds from the affairs were directed to "ongoing programs, the Swimming Pool Building Fund, and to the expansion of programs to meet the community needs."

Women Unlimited Committee
Front row: Brenda Williams, Mary Harris, Unknown, Dorothy Goodwin, Kris Felling, Linda Hoolehan. Bask Row: Joann Cerny, Susie Dinkel, Sherry Dekker, Jeannie Fagg, Mary Ollendick, Marcia Forsythe.

International Interlude - 1982

Facility Expansion Needed Again

By 1985 the building at Fairbanks Park was not yet ten years old and was being tested by the growth of the YWCA. The YWCA's summer newsletter reported that more than 130 activities and services were available to women and their families in Vigo and surrounding counties. With 3,393 voting members and participants, the need for a facility expansion was apparent.

On-Site Program

In April 1986, the YWCA started a pilot program in five workplaces to share information about services offered by the YWCA and the needs of women in the community. The YWCA On-Site Representative Program linked at least one volunteer from the workplace to be the source of information about the YW and its services.

The On-Site representatives met once per quarter at the YW. One of the first activities that evolved from the On-Site Program was the Lunch Hour Specials, a cooperative effort of the YWCA and others, such as IMC Pitman-Moore, Inc. employees.

Dorothy Jerse w/Pittman Moore Representative

Another spin-off was the celebration of Women in the Workplace, first held in 1987. Dorothy Jerse, executive director, announced that 368 women had participated in the celebration in 1989. In 1990, 125 workplaces were represented in the On-Site program. In 1996, the annual celebration became the Women for Women Banquet. It was held in April or May each year and became a major attraction for those eager to hear nationally known women speak on pertinent topics.

Women-to-Women Planning Committee:
Linda Hoolehan, Kim LaGrange, Susan Hayhurst, and Becky Buse

The presenters at the Women for Women banquet were women who had positions of leadership and influence in a variety of women's issues, from finance to politics to advocates for human rights and social progress. Notable speakers in the late 90s included Ann Richards, governor of Texas; Helen Thomas, UPI White House Bureau Chief; and Coretta Scott King, president and CEO of the Atlanta-based Martin Luther King, Jr. Center for Nonviolent Social Change. These banquets drew large crowds and were a significant fundraising event. A reception for Ann Richards sponsored by Terre Haute First Financial Bank in 1996 generated $7,500 toward several programs of the YW, such as Working Women's Clothes Closet, English as a Second Language, and the Y-Teens program. (See Appendix F for more information on Women-for-Women speakers.)

Women for Women Banquet

Networking

For the entire existence of the YWCA, a major benefit offered to members was that of networking. In 1980 during National YWCA Week, Sara-Alyce Wright, national executive director of the YWCA, when speaking of the YWCA stated, "We are a network of women on the move in today's world – an organization of two million women run by women for women."

The YWCA's definition of a network was a collection of activities, classes, and programs that had the potential to bring a wide variety of women together with a common interest – a common interest that could lead to endless combinations of other interests and collaborations.

Beginning in 1983, the Terre Haute YWCA reached out to neighboring communities to serve as many women as possible. YWCA programs were conducted in Clinton, Sullivan, and Marshall, Illinois, with plans to include Rockville and Brazil. Difficulties prevented Rockville and Brazil's locations from materializing.

To promote networking, on October 25, 1986, TV talk show host Sally Jessy Raphael, spoke on "Success and Self-Fulfillment – A Love Story." The event was co-sponsored by the YWCA and WTHI-TV and held at Woodrow Wilson Junior High School.

Examples of other networking events scheduled by the YWCA in 1986 included:

"Women's Breakfast at the YWCA" – 3rd Wednesday of each month.

"Women in Business" luncheons – 1st Thursday of each month.

"International Network for Women" – meetings held at Indiana State University Family Housing Community Center.

YWCA Membership

The benefits of membership were advertised for the 1987 membership drive as follows: becoming a member of the largest women's organization in the world, receiving a quarterly newsletter for program updates, discovering leadership opportunities through volunteering, and voting membership entitling input into programs and activities. Membership is honored at any YWCA in the United States and 83 countries around the world. Membership supports goals and programs, but is not a fee for services. Local membership dues were $15 per year in 1987.

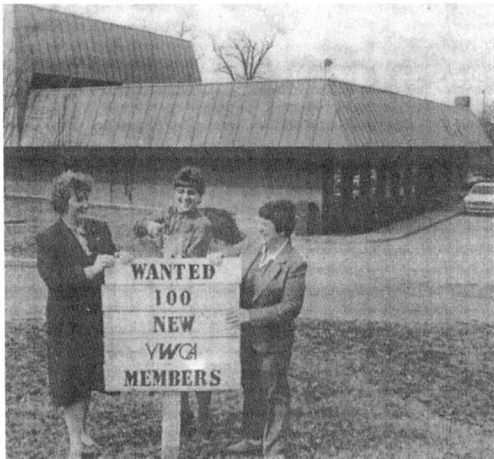

Membership Committee:
Donna Bolin, Liz Tuttle and Mary Add Baker, Chair

Need for Space

Dorothy Jerse, executive director, announced in 1987 that membership totaled over 4,000, with 2,600 adults, 500 teenagers, and 900 children under the age of twelve. The Terre Haute YWCA ranked second in size of the YWCAs in Indiana.

The large number of users caused every room to become multipurpose. A small fitness center was created, and 73 additional locations around the city were in use for programs and activities by 1988. One example of "an off-site program" was the cooperation of the YWCA with the Albert Pick Motel pool for swimming activities. Such off-campus programs had a history with the YWCA. For example, in 1975, three *Kiddy Kamps* were held in the Trinity Lutheran Church, the Central Christian Church, and the United Methodist Temple.

Raising Funds for Expansion

The campaign to raise money for the expansion of the YWCA was kicked off in 1987. Co-chairs Harriet Darrow and Joy Hulbert announced a major contribution from Chapman Root and his wife Susan of $500,000. The size of the gift was purposely large to encourage others to contribute.

Dorothy Jerse contributed the following in October 2021:

> **"On October 14, 1987, Marion Underwood, head of the local Coca-Cola business for years and a member of the YWCA Board of Trustees, wrote to Chapman about our plans for an expanded building and fund drive. We were hoping for his response as every fund drive needs a large gift to get it going. AND one Friday afternoon, the mailman brought a regular white envelope with a $500,000 check enclosed. Chapman's note read, 'I wish I could give more.'"**

Chapman Root

Henry P. Smith, son of the third president of the board of trustees, added $75,000 to an earlier donation of $25,000. Nearly 1,000 contributors added more to the growing account. Those contributing between $1,000 and $1,999 signed a tile which can be seen on a wall near the pool.

In February 1989, Kathy Perry, YWCA president from 1985-86, served as co-director of the fund-raising campaign with Mary Add Baker. They announced an anonymous gift of $200,000 with another $200,000 promised if the YW raised a matching $100,000 by May 1, 1990. Perry expressed confidence that the chances of raising the matching funds were excellent.

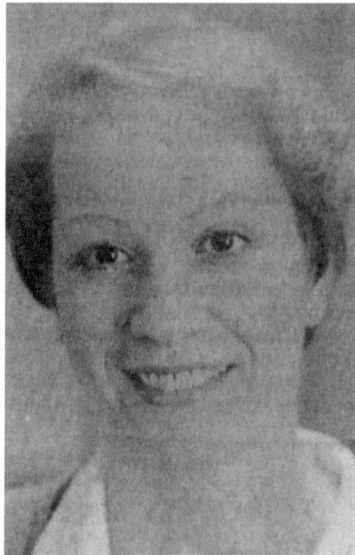

Kathy Hux Perry

Donnelly Directory had already made a $10,000 contribution. The $200,000 gift raised the total in the expansion fund to over $1,300,000, and as a result, the trustees raised the campaign goal to $1.9 million from the previous $1.5 million. One month before the dedication ceremonies, the committee for the Indiana Chemical Trust, on behalf of Mary Fendrich Hulman and Mary Hulman George, contributed $300,000 to raise the final total to $2,043,922, more than enough to finish the planned expansion and provide for furniture and equipment.

Mary Fendrich Hulman

Winter Walks

During the late 1980s and into the 1990s, the YWCA sponsored Women's Winter Walks. These events were scheduled in January each year to raise funds and to "celebrate winter and develop a positive attitude." In 1994, the walk, co-sponsored by Linda Burger, one of the strongest supporters of the YWCA, and Ann Lee Chalos-McAleese, began at the Medical Arts Building on South Sixth Street and ended at Burger Chrysler-Plymouth on South Third Street. The 1994 walk attracted 108 women participants. Other walks started at Meadows Shopping Center, extended to Deming Park, and returned to the shopping center.

Winter Walk

Breaking Ground

The Terre Haute YWCA broke ground for its $1.9 million building expansion on May 16, 1989. Dr. Harriet Darrow and Joy Hulbert were building expansion campaign co-chairs. Kathy Hux Perry and Mary Add Baker were fund-raising co-directors. Janet Pickett, campaign fund coordinator, and more than 100 volunteers, had worked to reach the goal of a debt-free facility.

Ground Breaking
May 16, 1989

YWCA
TERRE HAUTE, IND.

NATATORIUM &
GYMNASIUM ADDITION
1989

DESIGN SERVICES CONTRIBUTED;
    CONSTRUCTION CONSULTANTS, INC. Architects
    B & A Electric, Inc.
    SMC, Inc.
    Sycamore Engineering, Inc.

SUPERVISION SERVICES CONTRIBUTED;
    MARSH, INC. Architects
    Ralph Dinkel, P.E.
    Vern Fellows, P.E.

CONTRACTORS; HANNIG CONSTRUCTION, INC. General Contractor
SUBCONTRACTORS; Plant Brothers, Excavating
    Wabash Valley Asphalt
    Carey Concrete Corporation
    H. R. Barton, Masonry
    Benchmark Metal Products
    Hartman Company, Roofing
    Kasameyer Glass
    Commercial Flooring
    MAB Paints
    Lee Company, Inc.
    B & S Plumbing & Heating
    SMC, Inc. Sheet Metal
    AAA Electric
    L & W Pools

Contractors for
1989 expansion

Gymnasium Under Construction

Related Materials

YWCA On-Site Representatives

Sue Thompson--AAA Sewing Suite
Jeannene Secrest--Alternative School
Susan Butts--American States Ins. Co.
Maria Hartwig--American Cablevision
Denise Smith--Ampacet
Susan Rukes--Applied Computing Devices, Inc.
Sally Massey--AP&S Clinic
Elizabeth Art--Art House
Tiffanee Wilson--Associated Psych.
Alyce Williamson--Robert W. Baird Co., Inc.
Joan Barr--J. L. Barr Accounting, Inc.
Shirley Matherly--Bemis Co., Inc.
Becky Buse--Big Brother-Big Sister
Tina Keller--Brames Abel & Oldham
Betty Heine--Bridal Cottage
Lynda Drake--Brown Jewelry, Sullivan
Bunky Schupp--Century 21-Tom Thompson
Loretta Conley--TH Chamber of Commerce
Jean Wilkinson--Char-la Awards
Donna Sawyers--Charter Hospital
Norma Beymer--Chauncey Rose Junior High School
Carolyn Kumpf--Clay County Schools
Donna Bolin--Coldwell Banker-Larry Holman
Lela Carnell--Wayne Collins Real Estate
Phylis Fouts--Columbia House
Karen Keenan--County Market
Eileen Lantz--Covered Bridge Spec. Ed. Dist.
Carla Gore--Credit Bureau of Terre Haute
Linda Hart--D.A.D.C
Nancy Watson--Dairy Queen
Margaret Bruning--Davis Park Elementary School
Carol Cox--Devaney Elementary School
Sherry Lamb--Dixie Bee Elementary School
Jean Hiatt--Donnelley Directory

Jill Hoffman--Dove Specialty Advertising
Maureen Gwin--Elder-Beerman
Judy Krischak--Fayette Elementary School
Barbara Hendricks--Federal Express
Patti Holmes--Forrest Sherer, Inc.
Connie Garrison--Eaton Fuson Cadillac
Betty Kneller--General Telephone
Nancy Schoonover--General Housewares
Kim Smith--Girl Scouts Covered Bridge Council
Billie Frazer--Glas-Col Apparatus Company
Linda Worthington--Graphic Edition
Alice Hanson--Hamilton Center
P. J. Ekstrom--Vigo Co. Health Dept.
Virginia Clark--Hercules, Inc.
Linda Baxter--Honey Creek Junior High School
Mary Hood--Hood Watch Shop
Aletha Carter--I.S.U. School of Business
Sam Shanks--I.S.U. Federal Credit Union
Rosemary Zink--Indiana State Bank
Peggy Wessol--Ind. Dept. of Emp. & Trng.
Cindy Andrews--Indiana Business College
Kathy Shields--International Tours
Jill Hathaway--Internal Revenue Service
Candi Chubb-Wymer--Ivy Tech
Jan Edwards--J.C. Penney
Fredia Haviland--Kelly Services
Anne Stewart--Kroger Co. (North)
Darla J. Jones--Kroger East
Debbie Ogle--Kroger Co. (South)
Shirley Vester--Laughrey Bros. Roofing & Siding Co.
Blanche Law--Lee Co., Inc.
Brenda Thomas--Eli Lilly & Company
Ann Bennett--Lost Creek Elementary School
Mary Lou Quick--MAB
Jayne Cash--Manpower Temporary Services
Charlotte Manuel--Manuel Studio

Cindi Jones--Mid American Telephone Supply
Joan Abegg--Meadows Elementary
JoAnn Rogers--Merchants National Bank
Marilyn Wheeler--North Light Frame Shop
Jackie Moore--North Vigo High School
Susan Rozgony--Otter Creek Junior High School
Janie Poths--Ouabache Elementary School
Janna Toney--Petticoat Junction
Carolyn Wilson--Pitman-Moore
Kellie Johnson--Preferred Home Health Care
Ann Prox--Prox Co. Inc.
Karen Prose--P.S.I.
Carol Turner--Purdue Extension Services, Vigo Co.
Susan Baker--Quality Homes Realtors
Beverly Cristee--Horizon Properties
Pat Anslinger--Remax Real Estate
Marty Hillenbrand--Repcat Boutique
Jeanette Huffman--Riley Elementary School
Joyce Kemp--Rio Grande Elementary School
Carol Wetherell--Rose Hulman
Jerry Stultz--Royal Oaks Rehabilitation Center
Patricia Thoms--Sarah Scott Junior High School
Karen Eldridge--Sears
Linda Trusty--Sewing Basket
Elizabeth Trimpe Meyer--Shourson,Lehman, & Hutton
Connie Loveall--South Vigo High School
Susan Grusham--St. Mary of the Woods College
Mary Jo Taylor--Standard Register Company
Kim Streeter--Visiting Nurse Assoc.
Marsha Jackson--Sugar Grove Elementary
Barbara Rotramel--Sullivan Co. SW Sch. Corp.
Julie Pierce--Sullivan Peoples State Bank
Sue Kraemo--Sunset Harbor
Margaret Boyer--Sycamore Agency

Mary Lou Albert--Terre Haute Medical Lab, Inc.
Nancy Dene--TH Automated Flight Service Station
Sally Whitehurst--TH First National Bank
Stephanie Phillips--Terre Haute Housing Authority
Rita Coleman--Terre Haute Parks Dept.
Lori Price--Terre Haute Savings Bank
Linda Storey--Tri-Industries
Patty Krapesh--Tribune-Star
Paula Clark--Union Hospital
Debbie Norvanis--US Postal Service
Mary Ellen Christeson--U.S. Penitentiary
Ellen Aleshire--Valley Bank
Norma Coleman--Vigo County Public Library
Darlene Norman--Vigo Co. Park & Rec. Dept.
Pat Mansard--Vigo County Clerk
Mary Jane Compton--Visquesney's
Linda Snyder--WBAK-TV
Patty Brown--WCIEDD, Inc.
Donna Middleton--Weight Watchers of Central IN
Marjorie Burton--Vigo Co. Welfare Dept.
Margaret Hoggatt--West Vigo High School
Charla Burns--West Vigo Elementary
Debby Hickman--West Vigo Middle School
Nellie Eddy--Western IN Private Industry Council
Carolyn Tingley--Weston Paper & Mfg. Co.
Judy Critchlow--White Rabbit Copy Center
Gail Hayes--Williams Company
Janet Volkers--Williams & Assoc.
Dee Heine--Woodrow Wilson Jr. High School
Terri Williamson--Wilson Insurance Agency
Marilyn Pendergast--Woodburn Graphics, Inc.
Tammy Terry--WTHI-TV

Donor Wall
1989 contributors
(Fairbanks Park)

Mary Add Baker - Linda Hoolehan - Brenda Williams

During the early 80s, several YWCA women spent significant amounts of time in the YWCA kitchen during the Holiday Luncheon and Craft Week. These celebrations generated revenue and a great deal of comradery among the members. For the luncheons, all food was donated. All the ingredients for the turkey salad, green beans, cranberry sauce, and rolls came from various merchants in Terre Haute. Local restaurants donated pies and cakes. Later, a Holiday Cake Bake contest produced cakes for the dessert course. Board members prepared and served the food.

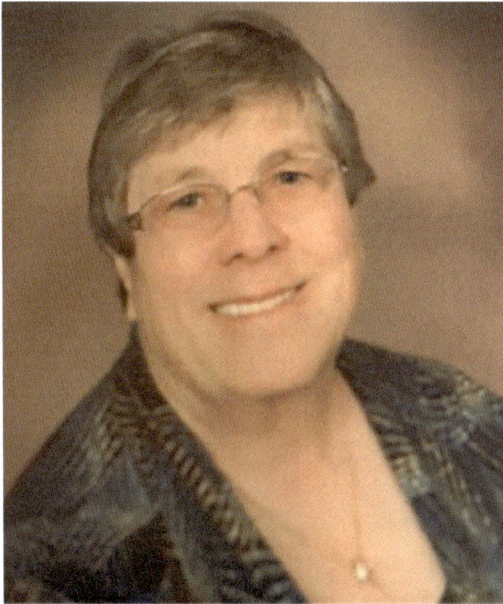

Mary Add Baker

There were three luncheons held during the week. One hundred twenty-five persons were served at each luncheon. One luncheon included a style show following the meal. The Holiday and Craft Week was scheduled during the last week of November or early December to avoid conflict with the United Way Fund Drive, which ended in late November.

A Bazaar accompanied the week-long event, which opened on Monday and ran through Friday. The bazaar usually had from 75 to 100 vendors. A bake shop selling homemade pies, cakes, bread, cookies, and fudge added to the offerings. A Patron's Night was held on the preceding Sunday evening for those giving a $5 donation to preview the event and shop early. During Patron's Night, committee members and volunteers would provide homemade hor d'oeuvres and punch to those attending.

Turkey Salad for 125

Turkey 4/10 pounds uncooked, per person

Grapes 8 ½ pounds seedless, halved, white or red

Celery 10 stalks, chopped

Pineapple 10 20-oz. cans, drained

Mandarin Oranges 14 11-oz. cans drained

1 Gallon Total of Mayonnaise and Miracle Whip (½ gal. each)

Mix above ingredients
Add lemon juice, ground ginger, and salt to taste
Serve on a lettuce leaf, topped with slivered almonds
(29 oz. almonds for 125 servings) and a sprinkle of paprika

Brenda Williams, an active member of the YW at the time, adds her memory of the event:

"The Y's gymnastics and ballet program brought me and many other mothers to the new YWCA. Friendships were forged in the hallways, and leadership grew from that base. The YWCA Board became filled with empowered women to make the Y a success. Thus, the annual Holiday Luncheon and Craft Bazaar was a well-planned fundraiser with the luncheon turkey salad prepared in homes, brought to the Y kitchen, and served in the gym

dining area. Along with the turkey salad, green beans, cranberry relish, and rolls were served. I still make the turkey salad today."

At this busy time, a cake recipe contest was also held, with the winning recipe made and served at the annual Holiday Luncheons.

Other cooking events were common during the 80s. Linda Hoolehan, President of the Board at the time, recalls members and volunteers making, bagging, and selling crepes to help raise money for the YW. She remembers the crepes being in demand.

Linda Hoolehan

Banana Foster Crepe

4 small bananas
Lemon juice
2/3 cup packed brown sugar
6 Tsp butter
Cinnamon
3 Tbsp banana liqueur (optional)
3 Tbsp light rum (optional)
Vanilla

Slice and peel bananas. Brush with lemon juice. Melt brown sugar and butter – sauté bananas quickly, turning once. Sprinkle with cinnamon and drizzle banana liqueur over everything. Spoon banana mixture into crepes and roll. Heat rum until warm and ignite. Blend with any remaining banana mixture and pour over crepes. May be topped with whipped cream or ice cream.

Basic Crepe Recipe

1 ¼ cups flour
2 Tbsp sugar
Pinch salt
1 ½ cups milk
2 Tbsp butter melted
3 eggs beaten

Place all ingredients in blender or mixer and beat well. Let batter stand for one hour for more perfect crepes.

Ice Cream Crepe with Dark Chocolate

Fill Crepes with vanilla or French vanilla ice cream. Top with cream and shaved dark chocolate. Chopped nuts or fresh fruit may also be added.

Living/Food

Section C

Top recipes selected for

YMCA Holiday Luncheons Dec. 6-9

Garcia cops first place

Local 'pig out' benefits Heart Association

Holiday Luncheons
(Typo – "YWCA" for "YMCA")

Anniversary celebration
YWCA planning many activities this fall as it celebrates 90 years in Terre Haute

YWCA Music Program begins; preschool accepting students

YWCA on-site program seeking new members

Mary DeBard directs Vigo County Y-Teens

Open House

DATE: WEDNESDAY, SEPTEMBER 3, 1980

TIME: 6.00 to 8:00 P.M.   YWCA

PLACE: 951 DRESSER DRIVE
in FAIRBANKS PARK

COME AND SEE A SNEAK PREVIEW OF OUR **FALL PROGRAM!!** MANY INSTRUCTORS, AS WELL AS PRO-GRAM STAFF WILL BE ON HAND TO ANSWER QUESTIONS ABOUT OUR PROGRAMS AND THE Y.W.C.A. IN GENERAL. BRING THE WHOLE FAMILY, FRIENDS AND NEIGHBORS.

REFRESHMENTS WILL BE SERVED!!

Headlines from the 1990's

YWCA comprehensive music program includes drum, guitar, piano classes

What Women are Doing: YWCA sets gourmet dinner dance for June 6

YWCA Junior Day Camp continues

Magic lessons offered at YWCA

Reservations accepted for YWCA dinner, dance

YWCA plans museum trip

YWCA preschool purchases equipment

Headlines from the 1980's

Chapter 7 Enjoying the Fairbanks Facility
The 1990s

Seamon print of YWCA

The Grand Opening

"Celebrate a New Beginning" was the theme for the Grand Opening of the building expansion of the YWCA in Fairbanks Park. Twenty-five thousand square feet had been added to the original 12,000 square foot building. The project included a five-lane swimming pool, a new gym, locker rooms, and a child care center. The new facility was impressive because of substantial gifts from local individuals and businesses exceeding $2 million. Following is a partial list of the most notable donations, as detailed in an article published in the *Tribune-Star*.

A gift from Mary and Ralph Barkley provided funds to renovate the main office. The gymnastics room was dedicated in honor of Breanne and Alyssa Perry and Kelsey and Molly Martin. They provided space for gymnastic equipment that had been used in parts of the old gym.

The gift of Chapman S. Root and his wife Susan provided a natatorium with showers for the handicapped, a pool ramp for seniors, and a computer-controlled monitoring system for water conditions.

Pool with Kids

The new gymnasium, named in honor of Mary Fendrich Hulman, was a gift on behalf of Mrs. Hulman and Mary Hulman George by the committee for the Indiana Chemical Trust. The gymnasium was large enough to accommodate two full-court games with enough room on the sidelines for spectators.

The day-care space that had occupied the dance room would be moved to the Sarah Elizabeth Smith Youth Center. This center was the gift of Henry P. Smith and Donald and Robert Smith in memory of their mother, grandmother, and third president of the YWCA board of directors.

The Oakley Foundation financed a dedicated place for the use of the Y Teens.

Honoring Susan Root
Becky Buse, Susan Root, Ann Prox

In August, a week-long grand opening was scheduled with special events, guided tours, class demonstrations, and more. Sunday, August 19, was reserved for patrons of the YWCA, Monday was Sports and Fitness Day, and Tuesday was Aquatics Day. Good Neighbor Day was scheduled for Wednesday, Thursday was Senior Citizens Day/Y-Teens Night, and Friday would conclude with "Aerobathon."

Dorothy Jerse Retires

The nineties would begin with a new executive director. Dorothy Jerse retired effective September 30 after eight years of guiding the Terre Haute YWCA. An appreciation dinner was held in Hulman Center on September 21, 1989, for the community, especially the YW community, to honor Jerse, who had been instrumental in guiding the YW through many of its successes. Approximately 400 well-wishers attended the retirement event.

Shortly after Dorothy Jerse moved to Terre Haute with her family in 1964, she took an active role in community organizations. She volunteered with the Boy Scouts and Girl Scouts in 1969. She was an Assistant Welcome Wagon Hostess (1968-1970), YWCA Youth/Teen Director (1970-74), Vigo County Historical Society Curator (1974-1982), YWCA executive director (1983-1990), provided radio commentaries on WBOW and WJSH (1990-94), and was a freelance columnist for *Tribune-Star, Terre Haute Living Magazine*, and other publications. She was the true definition of a "multitasker."

Her comments upon retirement:

> **"Terre Haute has been the perfect place for me to live and work. Here individuals can come to know persons of different races, religions, economic levels, ages, lifestyles, and even international students in a very natural way. What a contrast that is to suburban living, which limits contacts to persons very much like yourself."**

On the value of networking:

> **"I think networking is the answer to appreciating diversity and fostering understanding. We probably don't need any more groups or organizations, but those that we have, we must reach out to them. It has to be more than 'take someone different to lunch' once a year."**

On the YWCA:

> **"The YWCA is not about affluence of influence, but about women wherever they are. When people with different backgrounds come together, sharing ideas, growing, and feeling good about themselves, it is the most stimulating thing I can imagine."**

Unique to the Terre Haute YWCA was "Women in the Workplace," a program initiated by Mrs. Jerse. This program enlisted volunteers to be the YWCA representative in the workplace to generate program ideas for working women.

A major contribution of Dorothy Jerse's tenure was fostering a "can do" attitude. That culture strengthened the YW and led directly to the $1.9 million expansion, which tripled the existing building in 1990. Her attitude was summarized when she retired, saying, "We were told no women's group in Terre Haute could raise $1 million. . . . the expanded facility was opened without one cent of debt and I retired in 1990."

Comment from Kathy Hux Perry, past president of the Board of Directors:

> **"Dorothy was such an inspiration to us all; she provided us with the skills we still use today. She was WAYYY ahead of her time. I remember one year when about four of us went to a Convention in Chicago. Dorothy told us that she 'didn't want to see us during the day because our job was networking, and once we got back to our rooms at the end of the day, we'd all report to her what we'd learned.' Women in leadership was definitely what she stressed to us all and by example as well."**

Dorothy Jerse

A New Director

Martha Crossen assumed the duties of the executive director in mid-August. She left her position as an attorney and resource development director with the Legal Services Organization of Indiana based in Indianapolis. The new executive director stated that her background in research development, grant writing, and fundraising should mesh with her new responsibilities since the YW was still seeking funds for the recent expansion. Crossen mentioned that over $160,000 of pledges for the expansion were uncollected. She commented, "fundraising doesn't stop when the money is collected. One way to keep people active is to keep them involved financially, be supportive, and give them programs that are responsive to their needs." Crossen added that she had come into an almost ideal situation by acquiring a group of very YW-dedicated staff and volunteers.

Martha Crossen

New Board of Directors is Formed

YWCA picks new board

The YWCA of Terre Haute announced at the organization's recent annual membership meeting its 1991-1992 board of directors and officers.

New board members elected for a three-year term ending in 1994 are Pam Grimes, Mary Kay Jungers, Toni Schrimer, Margaret Woodsmall, Mary Fazekas and Jane Kohr.

The YW-Teen representative elected is Micah Howard. Howard, a Terre Haute North High School student, will represent YW-Teens for a one-year term.

Officers of the board of directors for the coming year are Mary Add Baker, president; Bette Jones, first vice president; Donna Middleton, second vice president; Ruth Baker, third vice president; Charlotte Nolte, treasurer; Carolyn Taylor, assistant treasurer; Martyne Graham, recording secretary, and Aletha Carter, corresponding secretary.

YWCA 1991 Board

YWCA celebrates Ninety Years

The YWCA's 90th year in the Wabash Valley was celebrated with a week-long schedule of activities in August 1992. The schedule emphasized the diverse offerings of the YW. Fitness programs and water classes were scheduled, health screenings were offered by Regional Hospital, the League of Women Voters conducted voter registration, Pat Mansard, Vigo County Clerk, spoke on "Women in Business," and seniors received a special invitation to sample YWCA offerings.

YW Teens

YW Teen groups, organized earlier, continued to attract junior and senior high school girls into the late nineties. The *Spring YWCA Quarterly* for 1996 listed community-caring projects for the previous quarter for each school YW Teen Club. Otter Creek Club made stockings, stuffed them with small gifts, and presented them to the Light House Mission. West Vigo Middle School Club held a bake sale to raise money with proceeds to sponsor a gift on the Angel Tree at Honey Creek Mall; the recipient received several new outfits. The Chauncey Rose Junior High Club made Christmas cards for Union Hospital patients. Sarah Scott Junior High Club made Christmas cards for a Vigo County nursing home. West Vigo High School served lunch for Grandparents Day. North High's ninth grade sang Christmas carols for residents of Lakeview Nursing Home and Rehabilitation Center.

Decorating the Pool

In March 1994, the YWCA announced plans to beautify the pool area. The walls were described as a blank canvas, and the YW held a contest to create a mural that would add interest to the surroundings. Anita Davis, aquatics director, indicated the entire 95-foot-long space was available with guidelines to be met by the final design. The subsequent mural remained for over two decades.

Mural – Pool Wall

Change in Executive Directors

In March 1994, Martha Crossen resigned as the YWCA's executive director to join Nellie Simbol at the law firm of Simbol and Crossen in the Tribune-Star Building.

Sandy Kyros was introduced as the newly appointed executive director of the YWCA on April 1994 at the eighth annual "Women in the Workplace" event. Kyros began full-time duties on May 1, 1994. One year later, she resigned.

Becky Buse

The *Terre Haute Tribune-Star* reported on May 22, 1995, that Andi Myers, president of the Board of Directors, was "thrilled" at the appointment of Becky Buse as executive director. Buse assumed duties on August 14. She previously worked with several organizations in the community dedicated to helping children's causes, most recently, Big Brothers Big Sisters. During her tenure, she oversaw the addition of a modern fitness center to the YW's facility and the updating and reopening of the adjacent softball facility.

Fitness Center Added

The spring quarterly of the YWCA newsletter announced that the construction of the 3,600 square-foot fitness center expansion was underway and would open in the spring. The fitness center was planned to "fill in" the southeast corner of the existing building. The ground level on that side of the building was elevated, which led to one plan to construct the center several feet above the floor level of the rest of the building. However, to maintain ADA compliance, enough excavation was used to lower the floor level to an elevation that would permit a small ramp to connect the old with the new.

In the same announcement, thanks were extended to contributors who raised $191,000 toward the goal of $400,000. The new co-ed facility would serve individuals over the age of fourteen, offering them new equipment to use. The existing equipment room was to remain for those who wanted an all-female atmosphere. The fitness center opened with a debt of approximately $90,000, but continuing efforts during the following year generated enough money to pay the debt in full.

YWCA building in 2000

Services of the YWCA

The YWCA was always characterized by the wide variety of activities offered to its members. The Spring 1999 Quarterly Newsletter announced activities for the upcoming season. The following is a condensation of those announcements.

Women for Women Celebration

Fitness packages for Introductory low prices

Golf Tournament

Herbal and Cosmetics classes
Aroma therapy
Herb therapy
Herbs for Kids
Steps to Decorating

Trips:
Nashville, Indianapolis
Gurnee Mills
Riverboat Casino
Chicago

YW Teens
Skating Party
Pancake Day

Land Aerobics Classes
Take a Hike
Body Sculpting
Conditioning
Step Aerobics
Co-ed Aerobics
Aerobics –Low Impact
Cardio Karate -- beginning
Advanced Cardio Karate
Martial Arts

Water Aerobics
Lap Swimming
Water Walking
Aqua Aerobics
Senior Splash
Private/Lap Swimming
Open/Lap Swimming

Personal Training Program
Massage

YWCA Super Kids Triathlon

Summer Day Camp

Spring Break Camp

Open Gym (walkers)

Teddy Bear Picnic

Summer Camps
Tennis Lessons
Karate Camp
Gymnastics Camp
(four different age groups)
Volleyball Camp
Golf Lessons
Girls' Basketball
Soccer
Cheerleading
Cheer Tumbling (10-16 yrs.)

Dance - Ballet -Tap - Jazz
Beginning
Intermediate
Advanced

Pool
Pre—Y—stars (3-5 yrs.)
Y – stars (6—17 yrs.)
Water babies and Tots
Private swim lessons
Swim team readiness

Related Materials

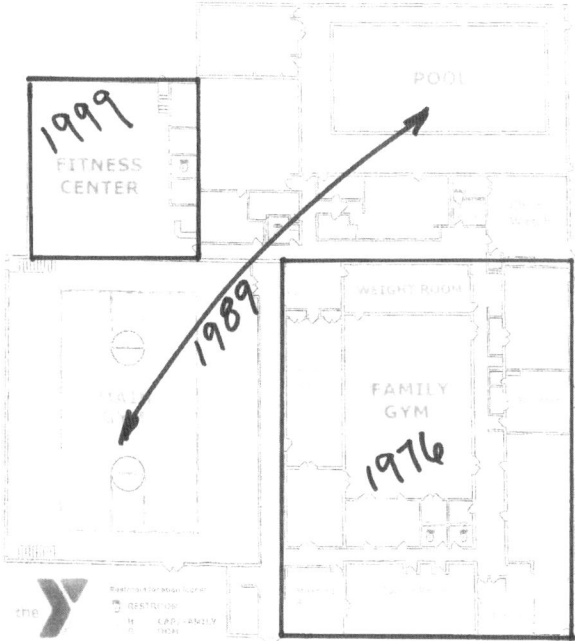

**Floor plan showing 1999
Fitness Center Addition**

Community
YWCA announces schedule of summer activities

YMCA to introduce new approach to aerobics Monday

Fitness Center fees listed

YWCA will continue Career Mentoring

YWCA plans grand opening of new building

Santa's elves call kids Saturday

Superstar Sitter program kicks off May 19 at the YWCA

Headlines from the 1990's

Tumbling among YMCA fall classes

Kids of all ages and with all direction and confidence. That is a noncontact league in wl

YW Teens keep busy schedule

Our Way program for mothers, daughters

The YWCA at 951 Dresser • Gramma's House — meets noon Nov. 12 in the YWCA. 1

Program focuses on types of walking

Winter activities abound at YW

YW-Teen's Sweetheart dance a 'blast' for Viking youths

Headlines from the 1990's

Chapter 8 Changes on the Way
The 2000s

New Board to Guide YWCA

2001 Board of Directors

Seated: Gail Thompson, Kay Newton, Martha Atkinson, Anna Hood, Carol Hutz, Claudia Tanoos. 1st row standing: Carolyn Roberts, Gladys Frankeburger, Kathy Dash, Rita Coleman, Bette Jones, Joplyn Kulhman, JoEllen Ornduff, Kathy Stone.

Back Row: Gerri Black, Betty Parsley, Krista Grange, Kim Eads, Judith Anderson, Cathy Grothe, Cindy Kinnarncy, Julia White, Donna McGregor.

Missing at time of picture: Mary Wright, Jennifer Hauley, and Genie Sanders.

100th Anniversary

The 100th anniversary of the founding of the Terre Haute YWCA was celebrated with an event at the Indiana Theater on November 16, 2002. A social hour was followed by a review of the YWCA's history with entertainment and slides. Narrators for the evening were Teresa Haverkamp and Beth Hughes, with Michelle Azar directing the music.

The YW's 100th year was also honored by the Indiana State Senate and House of Representatives. Included is a photo of State Senator Mark Blade introducing YWCA officials to members of the Indiana Senate.

**State Senator Mark Blade
and YWCA Officials**

Large Gift Received

On August 15, 2002, The *Terre Haute Tribune-Star* announced the largest single donation ever received by the YWCA. A $1 million gift for the future building expansion was presented from the estate of Ralph G. and Mary Barkley. Mary Barkley had been a "staunch supporter" of the YW through the years, from its move to Fairbanks Park in 1976 to its expansion in 1989. A portion of the $1 million gift was used to improve the softball field located adjacent to the YW building.

The following is an abbreviated account of the background of The Barkley Sports Complex and the Wayne Myers Memorial Field.

On October 12, 1963, the lease held by Commercial Solvent Corporation on a portion of Fairbanks Park expired, with control returning to the Terre Haute Parks Department. Don Coverstone, a local businessman, and Wayne Myers, a softball enthusiast, obtained a 25-year lease on the site. Later, Myers repaid the money Coverstone had invested and built the facility with the help of volunteers. A grand opening was held on April 28, 1964. Twenty-four years later, when the lease expired in 1988, an open-ended extension was granted until April 2002, when Myers "turned in the keys."

The facility was heavily used for much of its history. At one time, 23 teams played five nights each week with tournaments held on weekends. Terre Haute Softball Stadium produced 24 State Champions.

Wayne Myers died on January 10, 2010. A *Terre Haute Tribune-Star* article by Andy Amey called Myers "legendary." "At the local level, he was instrumental in promoting the Terre Haute Softball Stadium from its inception. As a participant, he was a Hall of Fame player. At the state level, he was instrumental in establishing Indiana as the preeminent state in the country . . . and at the national level, he served as president of the American Softball Association (ASA) for two years.

Myer's playing career perhaps was highlighted by his pitching duels against BoBo Bennett, father of Mayor Duke Bennett. Mayor Bennett said, "He and my dad often competed against each other. They were two of the best pitchers in the Midwest, maybe the entire country."

Myer's efforts were largely responsible for making softball a sport for women. From his efforts grew the Burger Chevettes, under the guidance of Helen Taylor. The softball team was a powerhouse, winning twelve championships in the Women's Fast Pitch Division.

To expand its sports offerings, the YWCA in 2003 leased the field from the Terre Haute Parks Department. Immediately, upgrades were made to the field, which had been largely neglected. The City Parks Department demolished the old buildings. Thompson Thrift Construction Company was contracted to build a new concession stand, lights, dugouts, fences, playground, and a new ball field. Approximately $250,000 of the Barkley grant was used for the improvements. The finished result was renamed the Barkley Sports Complex with the field's name honoring Wayne Myers – The Myers Memorial Field.

Becky Buse. executive director, stated in April 2004 "that in a few weeks, when improvements are finished, the YWCA would offer T-ball baseball for younger boys and T-ball softball for younger girls."

Myers Memorial Field

Slow pitch softball was planned for women and adult coed leagues on the main field. Cheryl Dorrough, YWCA sports and fitness director, said that a chance existed for fast pitch softball to return to the field as well. Later in July 2004, The *Terre Haute Tribune-Star* reported that Wayne Myers was again involved in organizing tournaments. A women's slow pitch tourney was scheduled for mid-July, a girl's twelve and under fast pitch tourney was scheduled for the following weekend, and a men's fast pitch tourney was scheduled for mid-August.

Programs continued for Young Members

In 2003, the YWCA offered the following programs for youngsters: "Musikgarten" for ages two and one half through six. "Move, Sing, Listen, and Play" with caregivers was for ages two to six to give first experiences with rhythm and tonal patterns. "Mommy and Me" class included art and music enrichment with outdoor exploration and a homemade snack. Another class offered during the summer session was "Bugs, Bugs, Bugs." Insect studies, stories, songs, and snacks were scheduled.

Day camps were offered for eleven weeks from June through August 2003 for ages three to six, six to twelve, and thirteen and fourteen-year-olds as counselors-in-training.

A program offered to the other end of the age spectrum was a grandparents' support group, which focused on empowering the increasing number of grandparents raising their grandchildren.

Leadership Change

Becky Buse, executive director, was appointed as a member of the Indiana Kids First Trust Fund Board by Senate Pro Tempore Robert D. Garton in July. She resigned from the YWCA on September 21, 2004 and was followed by Pam Weber.

Gymnastics at the YWCA

For the first 100 years, the most popular programs offered by the YWCA for youngsters were swimming, dance, and gymnastics. That popularity and participation in gymnastics peaked in the 1970s and 1980s because of the popularity of gymnastics at the international level. The competition at the Olympics, national meets, and even local college meets captured the attention of youngsters, especially girls.

In the mid-1970s, Patricia Buckner, YWCA Youth Director, announced the upcoming summer programs, including tumbling and gymnastics for boys and girls ages three to sixteen, with Roseann Callahan as the instructor.

In 1976, a program titled "Fit by Five" was offered to children from infancy to five years of age. Swimming and gymnastics classes were designed to develop motor coordination. Another interesting objective of the program was to encourage independence. Consequently, parents were urged NOT to be present during classes.

An indication of gymnastics' popularity was reported in the *Terre Haute Tribune* in January 1976. Twenty-two classes were scheduled for the upcoming eight-week sessions. As a result of requests from mothers of Roseann Callahan's classes, rhythmic gymnastics lessons were offered by Miss Shelly Harrison beginning in February 1976.

Instruction continued with ten-week sessions offered in the winter of 1977 for ages three to eighteen, instructed by Larry Rizzo, a former member of the Indiana State University gymnastics team.

Gymnastics Instruction

Gymnastic Students

The public demand for instruction in gymnastics continued, as indicated by The *Spring 1996 Quarterly Newsletter* of the YWCA. Twenty-six time slots were scheduled for seven different skill levels in gymnastics and tumbling. The popularity continued for several years. The *Spring 1999 Quarterly Newsletter* listed twenty-two different times for eight skill levels at Fairbanks Park and five additional classes offered at Central Elementary School in Clinton, Indiana.

Later the YW's offerings in gymnastics were substantially reduced. In retrospect, it appears that the rapid changes in the character of the YWCA beginning in 2006 and the closure in 2010 created uncertainty that caused many parents to look for other sources of gymnastic instruction.

Several Factors Led to End of the YWCA

After several years of financial stress, the Terre Haute YWCA and the Terre Haute YMCA combined resources in 2006 as a matter of financial survival. Both organizations had struggled for many years. Donna Roscoe, accountant for the YWCA for twenty-five years during the late 1900s and early 2000s, reported that as of December 31, 2005, "the YWCA was not in debt. The YWCA had several bills overdue, a small amount of ready cash, and a large trust. However, the trust was unavailable for operational expenses. The YMCA building at Sixth and Walnut in Terre Haute was closed, and both organizations shared the YWCA facility in Fairbanks Park."

Donna Roscoe has shared an opinion voiced by many passionate members of the YWCA community, "The YWCA contributed its staff, building, and equipment, but lost its name."

The YWCA, as an organization closed on February 9, 2006. After 104 years of continuous service in Terre Haute, the community no longer had an organization with a Y and W in its name. However, many traditional programs and services remained; others were discontinued or added as interests changed. Mission statements underwent revisions, but with some hiccups, it appeared that the essence of the YWCA would remain.

The *Terre Haute Family Y* was the name announced on February 9, 2006, for the new organization. Randy Wastradoski, former executive director of the YMCA, served in the same capacity for the new organization. On October 11, 2010, the *Terre Haute Family Y* disaffiliated from the YWCA and took the name *Riverbank Family and Fitness* with a mission centered on exercise and fitness. After two months of operation as *Riverbank Family and Fitness*, Tom Jones, board president, announced it would permanently close that day, December 8, 2010. The following two years witnessed several possible options for the use of the Fairbanks facility. In March 2012, a proposal from the Clay County YMCA was accepted by the Terre Haute City administration. After about two years of closure, the facility reopened with an open house on June 18, 2012, as the *Vigo County YMCA*.

Related Documents

YWCA
One Hundred Years
in Terre Haute

100th Year Anniversary Program

The YWCA of Terre Haute
Celebrates:

Women's Equality Day

Tuesday August 26, 2003

Equality Day Program

Becky Buse and guests at
Women's Equality Day

Epilogue

For over 100 years, the Terre Haute YWCA served the community by filling a variety of otherwise unfilled needs. These needs ranged from the lack of safe room and board for young working women to more recent needs for food and safety for children. Throughout the entire time, hundreds of classes, activities, and social opportunities have been available to all at minimum fees. No demographic of the community has been neglected. Programs for all ages, preschoolers to seniors, were offered continually, through good times and bad. Those offerings changed the culture.

The Terre Haute YWCA served two distinct functions during its existence. The first was the benefit of membership which included access to programs made possible by the physical buildings and the interaction of members, both as participants as well as leaders and instructors. The second function included various services offered to local and distant communities. These services ranged from child daycare to supporting members of the armed forces in times of war.

In conclusion, the YWCA was unique; it was not "just a gym." At the "YW," a family's grandparents could swim while parents worked on fitness, and their children participated in softball, dance, or gymnastics, with childcare available as needed. Clearly, these targeted activities filled an immediate need; time spent exercising benefited everyone. But maybe a more significant benefit was achieved at the same time. If a diverse group of people from the community met regularly at the same place, then mutual understanding, networking, and other unmeasurable interactions and activities provided important benefits to all. Will Rogers knew something about people. With leadership rendered by passionate YWCA staff, economic support from understanding community business leaders, and continual support from local agencies such as Community Chest and United Way of the Wabash Valley, the YWCA's accomplishments were countless.

Appendix A
General Assembly Act to Make Legal

YMCA and YWCA Associations in Indiana

Whereas, an emergency exists for the immediate taking effect of this act, the same shall be in force from and after its passage.

Whereas, A doubt exists as to the legality of the incorporation of the various Young Men's Christian Associations and Young Women's Christian Associations now organized throughout this state, and as to the right of such associations to hold real estate in their corporate capacity; now therefore,

An Act entitled an act to incorporate the Young Men's Christian Associations and the Young Women's Christian Associations organized in this state, providing for the election of directors, and trustees, the acquisition, holding and sale of real and personal property, exempting the same from taxation, regulating other matters connected therewith, and legalizing the organization acts and proceedings of all such associations heretofore organized under any law of this state, repealing all laws and parts of laws in conflict herewith and declaring an emergency.

Appendix B
Building Description

From an unidentified newspaper article
(Historical Museum)

FINALLY, Y.W.C.A HOME NEARS COMPLETION

Delays Cause Postponement of Opening, But Work is Progressing Rapidly

ADVANTAGES CAN BE SEEN

Rooms and Hall Are Being Finished in Attractive and Comfortable Manner.

Delays have made it necessary to postpone the formal opening of the new Young Women's Christian Association building nearing completion on North Seventh Street. It was hoped that the building would be ready for occupancy by October 1. The walls have been plastered, ready for the woodwork and floors.

On the first floor, the walls are to be tinted in shades to harmonize tastefully with furnishings selected, and the floors are to be of golden oak, beautifully polished. The woodwork throughout the building will be of red gum in the natural finish. The second and third stories are to have white hard maple floorings.

The first floor has a large central hallway opening into the parlors on the south. The front parlor is amply large for holding receptions with an adjoining smaller reception room.

The parlors are to be furnished by Mrs. Guy M. Walker of New York, only daughter of Mrs. I.H.C. Royse of North Seventh Street, president of the local YWCA. The walls in these rooms will be tinted tan shades, and the furnishings probably in the mission.

On the south facing Seventh Street is the private office of Miss Emma B Moore, general secretary of the YWCA. The office is divided into two compartments. [parts incomplete – The broad stairway is on the south side of the central hall . . . Just back of the stairway on the south side of the . . . is the library, a beautiful . . .] This reading room is to be furnished entirely by one of Terre Haute's young women. The walls are to be lined with bookshelves. In the rear of this are a large cloakroom and toilets.

The green tea room in the rear of the parlor is a welcome feature of the building, where dainty lunches will be served at private parties. The room will be attractively furnished and the China and service will be tasty. This will be rented out for private luncheons, teas and dinners. Between this and the kitchen is a serving room and the pantries, also a dumb waiter. The kitchen is large and will be most modernly equipped. On the east are the dishwashing room and refrigerator space. Provision has been made to serve three meals a day in the large cafeteria in the southeast corner of the first floor. This room may be entered from the large front hall and the kitchen. A noticeable feature is the good light, there being six large double windows on the south. The walls are to be furnished in the rough and tinted in a light green. The cafeteria will be furnished with 25 mission tables to seat four, allowing 100 persons to be served at one time. There are to be no waiters.

Auditorium and Stage

The second floor has an attractive auditorium with a seating capacity of 250. It is supplied with a stage, two dressing rooms, and a cloakroom. This auditorium will be rented out for musicals, and private entertainments, when not in use by the Association. There are five large entrances, and there will be folding seats. The remainder of the second floor is devoted to the domestic science room, a domestic art room, a public women's club room, a rest room, a general classroom, a transient guest room, two servants' rooms and baths. Scientific cooking will be taught in the domestic science room by Miss Annette Finley, a graduate of the Mechanicas' Institute, Rochester, New York. The Citizens Gas and Fuel Company has volunteered to furnish the gas stoves for this room. This course will be started by February 1. In the domestic art room, the members will be instructed by a competent teacher.

The women's club room will be utilized for the meetings of literary clubs and Bible classes. The general classroom will be used for any other branches that might be introduced. The rest room, located on the south, will be fitted up with lounging couches and will be for the working girl to rest during the noon hour. Provisions will be made to accommodate all transients.

The third floor is to be devoted almost exclusively to dormitories. There are twenty private bedrooms to rent. Each will be occupied by two girls in order to accommodate as many girls as possible. The rooms are furnished with two single beds, floor rugs, a dresser, chairs, and there is a large closet for clothes in each room. There will be general lavatories and baths.

Social Lobby for Girls

One of the most delightful features of the third floor is a social lobby located in the center, where the girls may congregate to read, sew, or be sociable. This general sitting room is well lighted with a number of small skylights. There is also a linen room on the third floor and a back stairway which leads to the trunk room in the attic. Miss Smith, the house secretary, will occupy a room on this floor. The basement is divided into a furnace and fuel room, the gymnasium and swimming pool, with dressing rooms, lockers, two storerooms for vegetables, four shower baths, one tub, and a well-equipped laundry.

The gymnasium dimensions are 36 by 55 and will be newly equipped with the most up-to-date paraphernalia. Miss Brown will continue as physical director, with an office in the front of the basement. The floors will be of white concrete. The swimming pool measures 18 by 36 feet, with a slanting floor of cement, the depth varying from 4 to 6½ feet. Classes of eight will be taken in swimming. The membership fee of the YWCA is $1 a year, and an extra charge will be made for the use of the pool and gymnasium. The charges will be $2 for four months in the evening classes and $4 for the same period in the morning classes. The building committee of the YWCA is composed of Mrs. I.H.C. Royse, president; Mrs. Jay H. Keyes, Mrs. L.S. Briggs, Mrs. Charles Brokaw. Mrs. A. Mack, Miss Moore, M.J. Smith Tally, A.J. Steen, I.H.C. Royse, and Mrs. Fred Smith.

Appendix C
YWCA Annual Report on Activities for 1956

Annual reports of the Young Women's Christian Association were mailed to members recently and gave a comprehensive report of the organization's activities in 1956.

In the division of the report devoted to finance, the major income was reported as $44,839.54 and the major expenditures of $44,846.43, with $210 withdrawn from capital funds in addition to the income items.

About one-third of the income, $15,659.20, is from the Community Chest, of which the YWCA is one of the Red Feather agencies. The residence of the YWCA housing 48 girls at a time provided $12,468.75 of income. The other major items in income were $9,452.26 in class fees. Other sources included community room rentals, food service, special gifts, and the bazaar.

Expenditures for salary and wages were $28,766.93; for supplies and services, $8,094.59; for building maintenance, $5,252.38; and for taxes and insurance, $2,732.53.

Report on Classes

During the year, there were 252 swimming classes with an enrollment of 2,003 and special lessons for six handicapped persons. Dance classes, free plunges, free swim and activities for young adults also were part of the health education division.

The 1,296 girls enrolled in Y-Teens participated in three play-days, "go-to-church" Sunday, and activities in their own groups, the 17 clubs in this department.

Eighty-three young women from 17 to 24 years of age and more lived in the YW during the year. Of these young women, 33 were office workers, 28 were students at Indiana State Teachers College, 27 were attending commercial college and beauty school, and six were in other activities.

A total of 25,648 persons attended the meeting of outside groups in the building, and 27,104 persons were served in the cafeteria. Attendance at YW meetings was 1,019, while 3,508 persons attended special YW events. Total attendance in YW health education and adult classes was 14,026, while 4,321 others attended the health programs but were not in classes.

There were 831 adult members in 1956 and 1,293 teenage members making a total of 2,129, nine greater than in 1955.

(This report was printed in *Terre Haute Tribune* on March 15, 1957)

Appendix D
YWCA Offerings for Adults

"Wabash Valley girls and women are the prime concern of the YWCA. A girl is a girl at the Y until she is eighteen; after that, she is a young woman and the YWCA continues to be concerned about her for the rest of her life."

Adult programs and activities as of March 18, 1973

The Residence Council

Indiana State University Student YWCA

Golden Age Club

Homemakers Club

Country Square Dancing

Matineers

Swimming

Golf

Trimastics

Mothers' jazz dance

Crochet

Bridge

French Country Cooking

French Conversation

Knitting

Needlepoint

Various Crafts

Triple Y

Single Parents

YWCA Collectors

Country Music Club

Day-At-The-Y

Armchair Travelers

Appendix E
Terre Haute YWCA Leadership 1902-2005

1902-1917 Emma Moore served as first General Secretary.

1902-1904 Mary Isabell Jenckes   President
(Title for Jenckes and Royse)

1904-1921 Sarah Royse   President

1921-1922 Winnifred Taylor   General Secretary

1922-1925 Julia VanArsdale   General Secretary

1925-1928 Mary Floyd   General Secretary

1928-1930 Minnie O'Toole   General Secretary

1930-1946 Dorothy Crawford   Executive Director

1946-1949 Hattie Campbell   Executive Director

1949-1960 Ernestine McDougal   Executive Director

1960-1973 Elizabeth Nattkemper   Executive Director

1973-1978 Eva Hopp   Executive Director

1978-1983 Karen Davies   Executive Director

1983-1990 Dorothy Jerse   Executive Director

1990-1994 Martha Crossen   Executive Director

1994-1995 Sandy Kyros   Executive Director

1995-2004 Becky Buse   Executive Director

2005-2005 Pam Weber   Executive Director

Appendix F
Speakers

Women in the Workplace and Women for Women Celebrations
The first in the series for Women in the Workplace.

1987 Sandy Rives

The celebration drew nearly 250 women to the Holiday Inn to hear Mrs. Rives, a columnist with the Terre Haute Tribune-Star. She spoke on the subject, "Swimming Upstream in a Goldfish Bowl." Rives said, "Women today are growing and changing, yet they are clinging to past feelings. She said women should take charge of their lives, accept themselves as they are, and believe in themselves."

1989 Susan Bayh - Indiana's first lady and legal consultant for Eli Lilly.

Mrs. Bayh spoke to over 400 in attendance at the Holiday Inn about her experiences balancing her roles as the governor's wife, legal consultant in business, and mother. She was an instructor at a YWCA for toddlers and was a strong advocate for adult literacy in Indiana. She directed her comments to the gathering concerning, "How women can better cope with their everyday challenges, how they can work to help make the environment a successful, positive experience for all involved and still keep their family life smooth (less bumpy)."

Susan Bayh

1990 Susan Porter Rose - Deputy Assistant to President George Bush (41) and Chief of Staff to Barbara Bush.

She spoke at Hulman Center on April 23. "I took risks, made moves from different cities, and made friends in new places, started at the bottom, started over . . . but I think it's worth it."

Susan Rose

1991 Janet Hauter - President of Summit Group International of Indianapolis

Topic: "Women as Transformational Leaders in the Year 2000." Hauter told the audience, "to inventory their strengths and concentrate on what will make them successful in the future. She said women have the right stuff to make things happen in the world of work."

1992 Harriet Miller - Executive Director of the Fort Wayne Women's Bureau.

Topic: "Challenge of the 90s – Smell the Roses. Miller told the group "to always remember the women who have helped them along the way – 'sheroes' as she called them." She added, "I don't want to see today's women work themselves to death as her generation did."

1993 Michele Edwards - 1991-1992 National President of Women in Communication, Inc.

She was a member of the Indiana Employment Training Council and Hoosiers for a Drug-Free Indiana, among other organizations. Her topic for the event was "Prescription for Change."

1994 Marianne Glick

President of Glick Management Associates, a firm she founded in 1986. Its mission was to train, develop, and motivate people to reach their full potential. She spoke on "Leadership of Women."

Marianne Glick

1995 Suzanne Green Metzer

President of Corporate Masters, Inc. An author, columnist, and adjunct professor at Indiana Wesleyan University. Her topic for the evening was titled "Being Positive in a Negative World."

Suzanne Green Metzer

1996 Ann Richards

First speaker for "Women for Women." Texas Governor from 1991 to 1994. Spoke at Hulman Center, where 1,230 were in attendance.

"Ann Richards, the smart, tough lady from Texas – a strong advocate for equality and balance between the sexes and races. Insists that no one be totally dependent on someone else for income."

Anne Richards

The YWCA of the Wabash Valley presents:

The Honorable Ann Richards

Wednesday, May 8, 1996

ISU Hulman Center • $25 per person

5:00 PM Cash Bar / Displays / Silent Auction • 7:00 Dinner

Co-Sponsored by Terre Haute First National Bank

Proceeds benefit programs of the YWCA

Table No. 91

Cameras & recording devices prohibited

Andi Myers, Ann Richards, and Becky Buse

1997 Helen Thomas

Journalist, Senior White House Correspondent

The eleventh anniversary of Women for Women dinner – May 14, 1997, at Hulman Center. Thomas had been named one of the twenty-five most influential women in America by the World Almanac. As a member of the UPI team, she closed each Presidential press conference with, "Thank you, Mr. President," a custom which continues.

Helen Thomas

1999 Coretta Scott King -- April 14, 1999, at Hulman Center

Born in Marion, Alabama, Coretta Scott received a BA in music and education at Antioch College. She followed that study at the New England Conservatory of Music, where she met Martin Luther King Jr., pursuing his Doctorate in Theology at Boston University. They married in 1953. During Dr. King's career, his wife occasionally substituted for him as speaker and often appeared on her own. After Dr. King's assassination, her time was concentrated on the Atlanta-based Martin Luther King Jr. Center for Nonviolent Social Change.

Coretta King

Coretta King and Linda Hoolehan

Rondrell Moore

2000 Dr. Ruth Westheimer - May 10 - Hulman Center

A popular TV celebrity of the time.

Dr. Ruth Westheimer and Banquet servers

Dr. Ruth and Becky Buse

Appendix G
Financial Support for the YWCA

For its entire existence, the YWCA had support from the community it served. Early on, major contributions came from the downtown businesses that enabled the construction of the 7th Street building. Until 1942, organizations seeking support conducted their own fund drives resulting in multiple, and often competing, campaigns in the community. Finally, in 1942, the efforts of many of the charitable agencies were combined into one organization called the Community Chest. The Community Chest had been active in the community for many years, but not as a consolidated organization. In its first year, $76,468.35 was collected and divided among the twelve agencies of the fund. The YWCA was allocated $6,300. As might be expected, the demands on the Community Chest began to grow immediately; the USO and the War Fund were added in 1943.

In the ensuing years, the Community Chest evolved into the United Community Chest in 1953, the United Fund in 1960 (serving 25 agencies), and the United Way of the Wabash Valley in 1972. In 2022, the United Way of the Wabash Valley, which serves several counties, consists of 110 agencies.

Samples of Agency Support for the YWCA

1953	$16,000	**1970**	$28,000
1960	$17,000	**1976**	$33,000
1966	$39,000	**1977**	$36,000

For many years the contributions from the supporting agency amounted to twenty-five to thirty percent of the organization's budget.

Image Source Notes

Chapter 1
Meeting a Growing Need: The Founding

Image	Source
Indiana State Normal YWCA	John Becker Collection
Indiana State Normal School North Hall	Indiana State University Archives
Indiana State Normal School 1918 Student Building	Indiana State University Archives
Jenckes Memorial	*Tribune Star* – (11-14-2020)
Mrs. I.H.C. Royse	Vigo County Historical Museum
Universalist Church	Vigo County Library
Cookbook Cover	YMCA Archives
Campaign Leaders	Vigo County Historical Museum
YWCA Building 121 North 7th Street	John Becker Collection
YWCA Gymnasium	Vigo County Historical Museum
Swim Lessons for Young Girls	*Terre Haute Tribune Star* (4-24-1966)
More Young Swimmers	*Terre Haute Tribune* – (5-24-1970)
Resident Dorm Room	Vigo County Historical Museum
Resident Dorm Room	Vigo County Historical Museum
1904 Board of Directors	YMCA Archives
Review of Accomplishments	YMCA Archives

Image	Source
Cookbook Liner Page 1905	YMCA Archives
Advertisements from Cookbook	YMCA Archives
Helpful Hints . . .	YMCA Archives
Indiana State Normal YWCA Cabinet	*1908 Normal Advance* (ISNS Yearbook)
Spectator Article	*Saturday Spectator* – (7-14-1996)

Chapter 2
Serving Communities Near and Far

Image	Source
Girl Reserves Cover	Vigo County Historical Museum
Girl Reserve Poster	Vigo County Historical Museum
Blue Triangle Logo	Vigo County Historical Museum
Switchboard Operator	Vigo County Historical Museum
Hostess House Cartoon	Vigo County Historical Museum
Fitness Cartoon	Vigo County Historical Museum
Cafeteria Opening	Vigo County Historical Museum
USO Group – 1943	Vigo County Historical Museum
USO Dance – 1943	Vigo County Historical Museum
Knitting Group	Vigo County Historical Museum
Sewing Group	Vigo County Historical Museum
WAC Sendoff Party	Vigo County Historical Museum

Image	Source
Muriel Allen	Private Photo
Overseas Wives Club	Private Photo
War Brides List	Private Photo
YW Teens	Vigo County Historical Museum
Harvest Moon Dance	Vigo County Historical Museum
Y Teens Group	Vigo County Historical Museum
Blue Triangle Ball . . .	Vigo County Historical Museum
Blue Triangle Girls . . .	Vigo County Historical Museum
10th Annual Report	Vigo County Library Archives
10th Annual Report – Inner Page	Vigo County Library Archives

Chapter 3
The Post-War YWCA

Image	Source
YWCA's Y's Urbans	*Terre Haute Tribune Star* – (3-9-1958)
Club 121 Members	*Terre Haute Tribune* – (12-11-1949)
Golden Age Club Meeting	*Terre Haute Tribune* – (11-18-1956)
Married After Joining GAC	*Terre Haute Tribune* – (4-17-1960)
Golden Age Club Officers	*Terre Haute Tribune* – (1-7-1968)
Food Service Closes	*Terre Haute Tribune* – (6-9-1959)

Chapter 4
Dealing with Disaster

Image	Source
Elizabeth Nattkemper	Family Photo
Girls in Street	*Terre Haute Tribune* – (9-19-1961)
Carl Ross	*Tribune Star* – (5-27-2013)
Tree Planting Ceremony	*Terre Haute Tribune* – (10-22-1964)
1968 Board of Directors	*Tribune Star* – (2-25-1968)
Four Generations of Swimmers	*Terre Haute Tribune* – (4-19-1970)

Chapter 5
Bursting at the Seams

Image	Source
Matineers	*Terre Haute Tribune Star* – (6-29-1975)
Church Tour	*Terre Haute Tribune* – (4-19-1970)
Day at the Y	*Terre Haute Tribune* – (4-19-1970)
Mrs. Venu Rathee and Mrs. Valda Kester	*Terre Haute Tribune* – (1-21-1977)
1975 Officers . . .	Vigo County Library
Cooperative Extension Mothers	*Terre Haute Tribune* – (1-11-1970)
Mrs. Jerse with Student	*Terre Haute Tribune Star* – (9-13-1970)

Image	Source
Ruby Daniels	*Terre Haute Tribune Star* – (11-2-1975)
Patricia Buckner	*Terre Haute Star* – (12-30-1073)
Junior Janes	*Terre Haute Tribune Star* – (4-23-1972)
Head Start Swimmers	*Terre Haute Tribune Star* – (5-24-1970)
Geraldine Bradford	*Terre Haute Tribune* – (8-8-1971)
Eva Hopp	*Terre Haute Tribune* – (7-2-1973)
Building for Sale	*Terre Haute Tribune* – (11-30-1975)
Groundbreaking	*Terre Haute Tribune* – (12-19-1975)
Residents Leave	*Terre Haute Tribune* – (8-16-1976)
Air National Guard helps . . .	Vigo County Library Archives
YWCA at Fairbanks Park	*Tribune Star* – (1-2-1977)
Landscaping	*Terre Haute Tribune Star* – (3-20-1977)
Original Architect's Plan	*Terre Haute Star* – (1-4-1976)
Floor Plan of Fairbanks Park Building Dr. Hopp with Junior Janes	*Terre Haute Tribune Star* – (9-3-1972)

Chapter 6
Programs, Programs, and Expansion

Image	Source
Dance Class	Vigo County Historical Museum
Kicking Up Heels	Vigo County Historical Museum
Stahley Article	*Terre Haute Star* – (10-3-1985)
Dancers	Private Photo
Dancing Down the Boulevard	Vigo County Library Archives
Women Unlimited Committee	YMCA Archives
International Interlude – 1982	Vigo County Historical Museum
On-Site w/Pittman Moore Representative	*Tribune Star* – (2-26-1989)
Women to Women Planning Committee	*Tribune Star* – (5-8-1996)
Women for Women Banquet	Private Photo
Membership Drive	*Terre Haute Tribune Star* – (4-5-1987)
Chapman Root	Museum of Arts and Science
Kathy Hux Perry	*Terre Haute Tribune Star* – (2-21-1989)
Mary Hulman	*Tribune Star* – (4-11-1998)
Winter Walk	*Tribune Star* – (1-10-1983)

Image	Source
Ground Breaking May 16, 1989	Private Photo
Contractors . . .	Vigo County Library Archives
Gymnasium Under Construction	Vigo County Library Archives
YWCA On- Site . . . (front)	Vigo County Historical Society Archives
YWCA On-Site (continued)	Vigo County Historical Museum Archives
Donor Wall – 1989 Contributors	Inside Fairbanks Building
Insert of Donor Wall	Inside Fairbanks Building
Mary Add Baker	Private Photo
Linda Hoolehan	Private Photo
Holiday Luncheons YWCA	*Tribune Star* – (11-9-1983)
Headlines from the 1980s	*Terre Haute Newspapers*
Headlines from the 1980s	*Terre Haute Newspapers*

Chapter 7
Enjoying the Fairbanks Facility

Image	Source
Seamon Print of YWCA	Authors' Collection
Pool with Kids	Vigo County Library Archives

Image	Source
Honoring Susan Root	*Terre Haute Tribune Star*
Dorothy Jerse	Private Photos
Martha Crossen	Private Photo
YWCA Picks New Board	*Terre Haute Tribune Star*
Mural – Pool Wall	*Tribune Star – (2-15-2006)*
Becky Buse	Private Photo
YWCA Building – 2000 Floor Plan	Duke Energy Photo
Headlines from the 1990s	*Terre Haute Newspapers*
Headlines from the 1990s	*Terre Haute Newspapers*

Chapter 8
Changes on the Way

Image	Source
2001 Board of Directors	100th Anniversary YWCA Newsletter
State Senator Mark Blade . . .	Private Photo
Barkley Field	Private Photo
Gymnastics Instruction	*Terre Haute Tribune – (10-28-1976)*
Gymnastics Students	Vigo County Library Archives
100th Year Anniversary Program	Vigo County Historical Museum
Women's Equality Day Program	Vigo County Historical Museum
Becky Buse . . .	Private Photo

Appendix F
Speakers

Image	Source
Susan Bayh	Private Photo
Susan Porter Rose	*Tribune Star* – (4-24-1990)
Marianne Glick	Private Photo
Suzanne Green Metzer	Program Photo
Anne Richards	YMCA Archives
Anne Richards Ticket	YMCA Archives
Andi Myers, . . .	*Tribune Star* – (5-8-1996)
Helen Thomas	Publicity Photo
Coretta Scott King	Private Photo
Coretta Scott King and Linda Hoolehan	Private Photo
Rondrell Moore	*Tribune Star* – (5-16-1999)
Dr. Ruth Westheimer. . .	Private Photo
Dr. Ruth Westheimer . . .	Private Photo
Dr. Ruth and Becky Buse	Private Photo

About the Authors

Pat and Dale Bringman are retired educators and are old enough to enjoy history. Pat taught elementary students during her professional career while raising two daughters and maintaining a home for the family. Dale's working career was spent teaching industrial technology courses at Indiana State University. They have lived on a farm near Terre Haute for over forty years enjoying gardening, cats, cows, and history.